Scriptures for th

ℒent *2005*
Savior on a Cross

A Lenten Study Based on the Revised Common Lectionary

David Kalas

ABINGDON PRESS
Nashville

Scriptures for the Church Seasons

A Study Book

SAVIOR ON A CROSS

by David Kalas

Copyright © 2004 by Abingdon Press

Scripture quotations in this publication, unless otherwise indicated, are from the New Revised Standard Version of the Bible, copyright © 1989 by the Division of Christian Education of the National Council of the Churches of Christ in the United States of America, and are used by permission. All rights reserved.

All readings taken from the Revised Common Lectionary © 1992 Consultation on Common Texts are used by permission.

ISBN 0-687-34560-X

Manufactured in the United States of America

04   05   06   07   08   09   10   11   12   13—10   9   8   7   6   5   4   3   2   1

Contents

Cover photo: Detail of Christ's head from *The Crucifixion,* by Mathias Gruenewald. One of the panels of the Isenheim Altarpiece at Musee d'Unterlinden, Colmar, France. Giraudon/Art Resource.

Introduction

Take a good look at the picture on the cover; the picture represents our theme; and, to a larger extent, the picture represents our faith.

The theme of our Lenten study, and of our cover art, is "Savior on a Cross." To those unacquainted with the gospel message, the image may seem an incongruous one. Savior on a cross? Isn't that like lifeguard on a stretcher? Or doctor on a deathbed?

The cross, more than any other symbol, represents our faith as Christians; and that is perhaps somewhat surprising. After all, we have many other options.

Countless people were crucified on crosses by the Romans, but only one person has been born God incarnate. Yet it is the image of his death, not his birth, that stands as the central symbol of our faith.

Likewise, every famous teacher, philosopher, and religious leader in history has died; but only one rose again. Yet it is the cross, not the empty tomb, that represents Jesus.

Many Christians around the world cherish the Lord's Supper as the central act of worship. Still, it is a likeness of the cross, not a chalice, that we put on our steeples, our necklaces, and our lapels.

We hold before us the life and teachings of Jesus as our model for how we should live. We find hope and joy in the stories of all that Jesus did in his ministry, from his gentle welcome of children and sinners to his powerful rebuke of demons and storms. Yet it is his death, not his life, that we commemorate with the ubiquitous symbol of the cross.

With so many other options—good options—why the cross? Perhaps because what stands at the heart of the gospel message is not God's power or glory or might but God's love. Perhaps because the startling part of the good news is not God's victory but God's sacrifice. Perhaps because, of all the great and good things that Jesus did, there is only one thing he did that saves me.

Take a good look at the picture on the cover. That image is our focus: not just within the confines of this Lenten study; it is the focus of our faith, our lives, and our witness. So, during the weeks of this study, we will take a good look together at our Savior on a cross.

The Biblical Drama

Scriptures for Lent:
The First Sunday
Genesis 2:15-17; 3:1-7
Romans 5:12-19
Matthew 4:1-11

It is all here. The three passages we consider during the first week of Lent comprise only a fraction of the Bible; but they are sufficient to introduce us to the cast of characters, the dialogue between those characters, and the basic plot.

While the pages of Scripture contain thousands of names, the biblical drama features just three main characters: the Lord, humanity, and the enemy of both.

The Lord, of course, is the star of the show. He deserves not only top billing but singular billing. The spotlight belongs on God and to God.

By God's design, however, the spotlight is shared with the co-star of his choosing: humanity. The biblical drama was not meant to be a tragedy but a love story; God's love invited human beings to center stage.

Finally, there is the villain. Truthfully, he does not deserve equal billing with the other two major characters. His importance is only derived from the degree to which he interferes with the two major characters and their relationship. He inserted himself into the spotlight, intruding into the otherwise beautiful love story with characteristic petulance and spite.

The plot, for all of its nuances, remains simple. The whole plot of the biblical drama is an extension of God's love. His creating, his warning, and his wooing in Act I are all products of his love. In Act II, God's incarnation and salvation are embodiments of his love. (Act III is yet to be played out, but we already have the script for it.)

Finally, there is the dialogue. Genesis 2 offers a snippet of the dialogue between God and humanity. Genesis 3 reveals the nature of the dialogue that always goes on between the enemy and human beings. Matthew 4 provides a rare peek into perhaps the most fascinating dialogue of all—the scene in which the enemy confronts God, who, at the time, is playing the part of humanity.

The cast of characters, the plot, and the dialogue is all here in these three passages.

THE MOMENT OF UNTRUTH
Genesis 2:15-17; 3:1-7

The instinct to say "I told you so" is generally an unbecoming one. Any phrase that everyone wants to say and no one wants to hear is a little suspect.

The problem with the saying is the element of gloating, of "I was right and you were wrong" that is so often involved. However, there are two virtues behind the phrase. One is the wisdom to be able to foresee what is ahead. The other is the concern to offer counsel and warning in advance.

God told them so. Before the subtle serpent ever got hold of Eve's ear, God had told them so. He had both the wisdom and the concern to warn them in advance about the one fatal fruit.

We will discover later, when we read the episode of Jesus' encounter with the devil, that his response to temptation was to quote Scripture. By that method, Adam and Eve had all they needed to rebuff the temptation, for they had God's word on it. The serpent, however, called God's word into question.

See how limited the serpent's repertoire is. There is no evidence that he could physically force or in any way coerce Eve to eat the for-bidden fruit. He had nothing tangible to offer her and no apparent power or threat to wield over her. He could only tempt, and his chief instrument of temptation was deception.

"Did God say, 'You shall not eat from any tree in the garden'?" the serpent asked Eve. That was not what God had said, and Eve noted that; but still the serpent had established its beachhead. We know from the world of politics the effectiveness of misrepresent-ing an opponent's position, of putting words in his or her mouth. Even if the misquote is refuted and corrected, it is still out there. The serpent planted a seed of doubt in Eve's mind about God's word and God's character.

Eve tried to clarify what, in fact, God had said. The serpent, how-ever, suggested that God was not being straight with her. It was not a consequence from which God was protecting Eve but rather a blessing that he was keeping from her. The risk was not Eve's—that she would die. Rather, accord-ing to the serpent, the risk was God's—that Eve and Adam would become like God.

It is ironic that the serpent should try to paint God as stingy and proprietary. God was, after all, the one who had given Adam and Eve everything. He was the one who had chosen specifically to cre-ate them in his image. They were already like God, a fact that the ser-pent must have found intolerable.

The script of the first dialogue between a human being and the enemy is tremendously helpful to us. The serpent is crafty, but it is not original. Its sales pitch is always essentially the same: raising doubts about God, telling lies, and encouraging those it tempts to go where God has warned them not to go.

The story goes on to describe what Eve saw and thought just before biting. Ever wonder what the fish thinks of the bait it sees? Ever wonder how the animal views the food in the trap? Eve "saw that the tree was good for food, and that it was a delight to the eyes, and that the tree was to be desired to make one wise" (Genesis 3:6).

Jesus calls the devil the "father of lies" (John 8:44), and we must recognize that deceit is its standard operating procedure. The serpent could not have sold its product—sin and death—if Eve had seen them for what they were. What Eve saw, however, was "good," "a delight," and "to be desired."

Before the Fall, it would have been useless for the serpent to tempt Eve with fallen pleasures. She could not be attracted to evil. In her perfection, however, she was naturally attracted to goodness, beauty, and wisdom.

It may be that the serpent continues to hoodwink the people of God in this way. We wring our hands about the obvious evils in society; and in the process, we overlook the ways that the enemy lures people away from God with things that appear to be good. Remember that it was not manifestly sinful, evil stuff that kept the would-be disciples from following Jesus (Luke 9:59-62).

As we read the story of this pivotal event in Eden, one wonders about the road not taken. What options did Eve have? What else might she have done? What could have happened as a result?

When people complain about offensive content on television programs, a common retort is, "You don't have to watch it. Just turn it off." While that policy does not address the concern for decency in broadcasting; at an individual level, it is an effective approach. No one can force me to watch something offensive. I have the control in hand; I can always just turn it off.

I wonder how often the same approach can be used with the devil. Since, apparently, it cannot force me to disobey God, I wonder if I have the capacity simply to turn it off. Just as I am surely a hypocrite to sit glued to the screen while complaining about how offensive it is, I am also without excuse if I linger around the off-limit tree engaged in a lengthy conversation with the serpent.

Not much can be said about Adam's encounter with the object of their disobedience. His surrender to sin is appallingly quick and easy. If Eve is to be faulted for considering too long the forbidden fruit, Adam is at fault for considering it too little.

John Wesley fills in the blanks of Scripture a bit, imagining what discussion may have taken place between Adam and Eve. "She gave it to him, persuading him with the same arguments that the serpent had used with her. And to this she added that she herself had eaten of it and found it so far from being deadly that it was extremely pleasant and grateful."[1]

Whether the discussion was long or short, Eve led Adam into sin. She was, to borrow a phrase we use casually, the "devil's advocate." The serpent had done its work personally with Eve. It did not need to do the job with Adam, for Eve took on that role. What a tragic perversion of the good thing God intended when he made human beings for one another. "Wilt thou forgive," John Donne laments, "that sin which I have won others to sin? and, made my sin their door?"[2]

Finally, see the human response in the wake of their sin. They endeavored to cover themselves.

The teenager with a pimple awkwardly keeps finding an excuse to cover it with a hand or hair. The man who realizes he has a stain on his necktie works hard to keep it concealed until he can correct it.

When we are unblemished, we are unselfconscious. However, our shame turns our focus inward; and we struggle to cover our unsightly spots from the view of others. We hide our junk in the closet or back bedroom and then keep our guests away from there. We wear clothes that flatter us and conceal our poorer features. We put on a façade, mortified by the prospect of someone discovering the ugly truth about us.

When Adam and Eve were without sin, they were without shame. As soon as they disobeyed God, however, shame became a reflex; and they sought to cover themselves.

Elizabeth Clephane, a Presbyterian woman in 19th-century Scotland, understood the problem. She discovered the antidote as well. "My sinful self my only shame, my glory all the cross."[3]

When have you been tempted to doubt the character or word of God?

What evils have been disguised as good things in your experience? What good things have drawn you away from God?

When do you linger around temptation rather than resist it or do whatever is possible to turn it off?

Have you ever led someone else into sin? What are some different ways that can happen?

What sin are you trying to conceal from others? from God?

WHAT ONE MAN CAN DO ... ONLY ONE MAN
Romans 5:12-19

Paul's epistle to the Romans is sometimes called "the gospel according to Paul." In this letter, the apostle offers his most complete explanation of what he believes and proclaims. Other epistles (for example, the letters to the Corinthians and Galatians) are so specifically geared to the circumstances of the audience that they do not have the scope and balance of what Paul writes to the Romans.

Unlike most of the churches to which Paul writes, the church at Rome had not been founded by Paul. These people were not his people. While he knew the church by reputation and knew some of the members there personally, his letter to the Romans is a letter of introduction. In anticipation of a visit to Rome, Paul wrote to introduce himself to the Christians there. As such, the letter is a rich treasure for us, offering a thorough explanation of Paul's understanding of the gospel.

Leading up to our selected passage, Paul has outlined the human condition of sin, the purpose of God's law, and the salvation offered in Christ. Specifically, he notes that all human beings are unrighteous—whether they are Jews with the Law or Gentiles without the Law. Yet, God makes us right with himself by the free gift of God's grace in Jesus Christ. That gift is provided by the sacrificial death of Christ, and it is accessible to all by faith.

In our particular passage, Paul offers an explanation of Christ's saving death. It is not an account of his death, such as we find at the end of each of the four Gospels. Paul does not point back to Calvary to explain what Christ did; rather, he points all the way back to Eden.

The Gospels tell the story of Christ's death in the context of the story of his life. Paul steps back and looks at the bigger picture. He explains the work of Christ in the larger context of the human story. It is a story that begins with Adam.

Paul sees a great symmetry in the relationship between the problem and the solution. The problem is sin, with its accompanying judgment and death. The solution is salvation, complete with justification, righteousness, and eternal life. Paul observes that both the problem and the solution came into the world by one man.

Sin came into the world by one man: Adam. His trespass led to death and condemnation for many. Salvation, likewise, came into the world by one man: Jesus. His act of obedience leads to the free gift of God's grace and righteousness for many.

Two key theological concepts are in play here. We see, first, the doctrine of original sin, that is, the understanding that all humanity was infected by the sin of their parents, Adam and Eve. Long before modern psychology identified patterns of dysfunction in family systems, Scripture identified the great dysfunction in the human family. Humankind, originally perfect and free, lived under the dominion of sin and death since the fall of Adam.

William Barclay observes that this concept may be difficult for the modern mind but that the ancient Jews accepted it quite readily. He cites the episode in which all Israel is punished for the sin of Aachan (Joshua 7) and observes, "That is how Paul sees Adam. Adam was not an individual. He was one of mankind, and because he was one of mankind, his sin was the sin of all men."[4]

The second great doctrine at work in this passage is salvation by grace. Humankind's condition would be hopeless and incurable were it not for God's grace. The Law could not save us from sin; it could only identify and tally our sins. Human attempts at righteousness were ultimately futile because we lived under "the law of sin and of death" (Romans 8:2). By the free gift of God's grace, however, the obedience of the one righteous man offers to make us all righteous and to restore to us a right relationship with God.

As he reflects on the free gift of grace, Paul declares that there is more to it than mere symmetry. While sin and salvation each came into the world by one man, what the one man Jesus did was far greater than what the one man Adam did. The gift is greater than the trespass, the dominion of righteousness far greater than the dominion of death.

Here, then, is a truth we too often forfeit. Discouraged by our sinfulness, we regard sin as the great inevitable. "Nobody's perfect" is our prevailing doctrine. We perceive grace and salvation as fragile and airy, while sin is the substantial reality in the world and in our lives. We relinquish most of God's salvation to heaven and the afterlife, concluding that sin is the constant in the here and now.

Paul's view is different. The grace, righteousness, and life offered in Christ are greater and stronger than the previous order of sin and death. The latter lie shattered and impotent in Christ's wake. What Adam brought into the world is no contest for what Christ brought.

Humankind did not play its part as God intended in the beginning. Even so, we could not prevent the story from being a love story, for God lovingly seeks and saves us from our sin.

What are the implications for you of God's grace being a free gift?

To what extent do you perceive and experience that God's offered grace and righteousness are stronger than sin and death?

If we are saved by Christ's obedience and righteousness, what role do your obedience and righteousness play in your salvation?

SHOWDOWN
Matthew 4:1-11

Matthew, Mark, and Luke tell the story of Jesus' temptation immediately following his baptism by John and just before he begins his work in Galilee. Characteristically, Mark's version is quite brief and lacks the detail and dialogue found in Matthew and Luke. Matthew and Luke, meanwhile, provide the particulars of the three specific temptations presented by the devil, as well as Jesus' response to each.

Luke's version suggests that Jesus was tempted for 40 days, while in Matthew it appears that the temptation occurred at the end of his 40 days of fasting. Though both Gospel accounts begin with the "stones into bread" temptation, they report the other two temptations in reverse order. Angels come to help Jesus following his temptation in Matthew. Matthew's account also includes Jesus saying, "Away with you, Satan!" (4:10) in his response to the third temptation.

It is interesting to note that Jesus addressed the enemy by name. As narrator, Matthew consistently refers to it as "the devil," which is more of a title; but Jesus called it by name, "Satan." There is a kind of grab-him-by-the-collar, authoritative quality in Jesus' use of the enemy's name. In calling the devil by its name, Jesus at once both identifies and dismisses it.

The devil, meanwhile, never tries to call Jesus by name. That, we can presume from other passages of Scripture (Mark 16:17; Acts 16:18; Philippians 2:9-11), it would find intolerable. While the devil tries to coax Jesus to bow down before it, the obeisance will cut the other way "at the name of Jesus." It is symbolic of the inequity between these two beings that Jesus can name the enemy but the enemy cannot speak Jesus' name. "One little word shall fell him,"[5] as Martin Luther sang.

We noted in our discussion of Genesis 3 that the serpent's only real ability was to tempt, and its only real instrument was deception—likewise, here in the wilderness with Jesus. There does not seem to be anything aggressive or coercive that the devil can do to Jesus. It can only tempt.

We are perhaps uneasy with the prospect of Jesus being tempted. If he, as God's Son, was somehow invulnerable to temptation, then we can discount the story; and it has little practical application to our lives. If, on the other hand, Jesus was genuinely tempted, then we are inclined to question his perfection. After all, doesn't the very fact that we are tempted prove our sinful nature?

Yet, the writer of Hebrews affirms that Jesus "in every respect has been tested as we are, yet without sin" (4:15). The Greek word translated "tested" by the NRSV here is the same as the Greek word used in Matthew 4 when Jesus was tempted by the devil. The message in Hebrews is that Jesus experienced temptation just as we do, but he emerged sinless.

Of course, that a person without a sinful nature can nevertheless be tempted is evidenced by the first passage, the story of Eve and the serpent in Eden. The serpent did not appeal to some baseness within Eve. She would not have succumbed for something plainly evil. Rather, he got her to bite when she perceived the bait as "good," "a delight," and "to be desired." In Matthew, the devil does not dangle before Jesus all manner of perversion and debauchery. Rather, he endeavors to tempt Jesus with plausible goods.

Bread certainly is not a bad thing. The traditional Hebrew table prayer recognized that it was the Lord who brought forth bread from the earth. If it is a blessing and a provision from God, how can it be sinful? All provisions for our fleshly appetites—food, drink, sleep, and sex—are gifts of God. Yet each one of them can be used out of turn or perverted so that it is displeasing to God.

In the case of the "stones into bread" temptation, it is unclear in the immediate context where the sinfulness lay. In the larger context of Jesus' life and ministry, however, we discover that he never used a miracle exclusively for his own benefit. Perhaps a temptation peculiar to the Son of God is that he would exploit his supernatural ability to indulge selfishness. In any case, Jesus put the matter into proper perspective: "One does not live by bread alone, / but by every word that comes from the mouth of God" (Matthew 4:4).

The second temptation in Matthew's account is perhaps the most diabolical. The devil, knowing full well who Jesus was, challenged him to prove who he was. That would be a continual temptation for Jesus (Matthew 12:38-39; 16:1; Luke 23:8; John 2:18; 6:30) as people sought signs and proofs. Even as Jesus hung on the cross, the skeptics cried out for him to prove himself (Matthew 27:38-44).

The particularly diabolical component of this second temptation is that Satan used Scripture in his appeal. It is always the nature of heresy to use God's word or God's work to draw people away from God. It is the earnest ones who are especially susceptible to this ploy. Those who are indifferent to God will not respond to a misuse of his word any more than to a proper proclamation of it. However, those who are eager to respond to God and his word make easy targets for the false prophet who cries out, "Thus says the Lord."

Jesus resists the temptation to prove himself, just as he did throughout his ministry. He knew that the real sign of his identity was yet to come (Luke 11:29-30; John 2:18-19).

The third temptation seems to be the most obviously evil—the invitation to fall down and worship the devil. Yet it is a classic "ends justify the means" scenario, which has compromised most of us at one time or another. What is at stake is no less than "all the kingdoms of the world" (Matthew 4:8). Surely it was God's will that "the kingdom of the world ... become the kingdom of our Lord and of his Messiah" (Revelation 11:15). This temptation promised to be a means to God's end.

In the Old Testament, we see young David reject two such shortcuts to God's will. Two different times (1 Samuel 24; 26), David, who had already been anointed to be the next king of Israel, had the opportunity to accelerate his coronation. King Saul had lost God's favor and lost his mind. He spent his time and resources trying to capture and kill David, who had been only loyal to him. Two times David had the chance to kill Saul, opportunities that David might reasonably have concluded were from God (1 Samuel 26:8). Still, David would not sin in pursuit of God's ultimate will nor did Jesus sin in pursuit of God's ultimate will. A shortcut for Jesus would have meant bypassing the cross, which is something Peter also encouraged. On that occasion (Matthew 16:21-23), as during his temptation by the devil, Jesus declared, "Go away, Satan!"

When the apostle Paul describes the armor of God (Ephesians 6:11-17), he identifies the word of God as the Christian soldier's sword (verse 17). In Matthew 4, we see that sword used to good effect by Jesus. Each temptation is answered from Scripture.

In Genesis 3 and Matthew 4, we see Satan's script. Its lines are always pretty much the same. In Matthew 4, however, we get a clearer sense of what our part of the dialogue should be. Jesus responds with Scripture so that, literally, God has the last word in each temptation.

We so often resort to lesser tools when trying to fend off or defeat temptation. The most common weapon of choice is willpower. What an odd selection! It reflects our tendency toward self-reliance, but such self-reliance is inadequate for our salvation.

In fact, most of us have discovered that the idea of willpower is something of an oxymoron. When it comes to sin, our will is a major part of our problem. So often my fallen will desires the thing that the serpent dangles before me. I put the mouse in charge of guarding the cheese when I employ my will to protect me against sin.

Better that I should go into battle against temptation equipped with God's will than with my will. If I am to win the battle, I must begin with surrender: I surrender my will to God's. My best path to God's will is God's word. Let that be the substance of my dialogue with the enemy.

How does it make you feel to know that Jesus also was tempted just as you are tempted?

Have you ever tried to take a shortcut to God's will or rationalized your decisions by saying, "The end justifies the means"?

How do you typically respond to temptation?

When have you employed God's word in resisting and responding to temptation? How might you employ God's word in responding to temptation in the future?

---

[1] From *Wesley's Notes on the Bible,* edited by G. Roger Schoenhals (Francis Asbury Press, 1987); page 27.

[2] From *John Donne: The Complete English Poems,* edited by A. J. Smith (Penguin Books, 1975); page 349.

[3] From Stanza 3 of "Beneath the Cross of Jesus," by Elizabeth C. Clephane (1872).

[4] From *The Daily Bible Study Series: The Letter to the Romans,* by William Barclay (The Westminster Press, 1975); page 79.

[5] From Stanza 3 of "A Mighty Fortress Is Our God," by Martin Luther (1529), translated by Frederick H. Hedge (1853).

The Name on an Open Invitation

Scriptures for Lent:
The Second Sunday
Genesis 12:1-4a
Romans 4:1-5, 13-17
John 3:1-17

I attended a funeral recently that was followed by dinner at a local restaurant. My past experience in this community had been that everyone in attendance at the funeral was invited to such meals. When the service was over, however, I had conversations with members of the family of the deceased; and none of them made reference to the dinner. No one asked me, "Will we see you at the restaurant?" or "Are you coming to the dinner?"

As I walked to my car, I was uncertain what to do next. Since no one mentioned the dinner during or after the service, I thought that perhaps I had misunderstood. Maybe there was no meal, or maybe it was just for immediate family.

I suspect that each of us has found ourselves in a situation where an invitation was unclear. We do not want to miss an event where we are expected, but neither do we want to presume on an occasion to which we are not invited. So we wonder what to do.

There is no such uncertainty in Scripture. The invitation extended by God in Christ is an open invitation. Everyone is invited. Everyone is welcome.

God's open invitation is epitomized by the familiar and cherished verse of Scripture we know as John 3:16. In the language of the King James Version that many of us memorized as children, Jesus says, "For God so loved the world, that he gave his only begotten Son, that whosoever believeth in him should not perish, but have everlasting life."

"Whosoever" is the name on God's open invitation.

MISSION STATEMENT
Genesis 12:1-4a

The Lord told Abram to go. You and I may be more attracted to the stories and teachings where the Lord says, "Come"; but here (as well as elsewhere) the instruction is, "Go."

The details of God's instruction to Abram seem almost cruel. He offers no specifics about where Abram is supposed to go ("the land that I will show you"), but he is painfully specific about where Abram is supposed to leave ("your country and your kindred and your father's house").

The trebled reference to Abram's home is reminiscent of God's later instruction to Abraham to present his son Isaac as an offering. When he made his unbearable request of Abraham, the Lord again used a kind of triple-reference: "Your son, your only son Isaac, whom you love" (Genesis 22:2).

The repetition seems unnecessary. Why does God belabor the point? Is it not enough to say "Leave your home" or "sacrifice your son" without harping?

On the other hand, perhaps we human beings are too naturally inclined to cling to what we have, what we know, and what we cherish. So, when the Lord and his work requires us to leave those people, those places, those things, his command must be unambiguous.

Furthermore, just as Jesus later urged would-be disciples to count the cost of following him (Luke 14:25-33), here too the Lord is eager to be clear about the price of Abram's obedience. Unlike the salesperson whose techniques make the price of his product

seem like a bargain, God does not try to coax Abram. God does not pretend that obedience will not cost Abram much. On the contrary, God itemizes the cost. Abram is being asked to leave country, kindred, and his father's house: that is, his place, his people, and his very roots.

Abram's challenge is a familiar one. We are always more familiar with what we are being asked to leave behind than we are with what God has in store. James and John could see and touch their nets, their boat, and their father (Mark 1:19-20); but they had no idea where following Jesus would lead them. Still, they went. So did Abram.

The Lenten season is an appropriately reflective time for us to count the cost of discipleship. While the portrait of salvation may be a picture of Christ carrying the cross, the portrait of discipleship is a picture of us carrying a cross (Luke 9:23). Time and again in the Gospels, Jesus calls on individuals to sacrifice in order to follow him (Matthew 16:25; Luke 9:57-62; 18:18-23). Abram is distant from us in time and space, but his story is not so far from our experience. We serve the same God, and that God calls us to leave behind what we know and what we have in order to arrive at the place that he will show us.

God did tell Abram something about the plans he had in mind for him. They were not the kind of near-future, practical details that typically concern us, however. He did not print out an itinerary for Abram. He did not provide for Abram a winsome description of the new neighborhood or a promise of how many bedrooms, baths, and square feet awaited them. Instead, God showed Abram the big-picture future that he had in mind; and it was big indeed. God's future for Abram was not confined to a house, a piece of property, or even a lifetime. Rather, remarkably, God's future for Abram involved the whole world. Self-interest may tempt us to stop and focus on God's plan for our lives, but that is a comparatively small matter when stacked up against his purpose for our lives.

God's plan for Abram, as described in this passage, featured three components: (1) becoming a great nation, (2) receiving God's blessings, and (3) having a great name. Notice, however, that God's plan is not identical with God's purpose.

The purpose clause in God's word to Abram is signified by the words "so that." Following God's three-part plan comes the statement of God's purpose: "so that you will be a blessing."

Mission statements are very fashionable these days in businesses, schools, and churches. Many people have even crafted and adopted personal mission statements. Here is Abram's lofty and lovely mission statement from God: "to be a blessing."

God promised to bless Abram, but he did not mean for that to be the end of the circuit. Abram was no mere repository for God's kindnesses; rather, he was ordained to be a conduit through which "all the families of the earth shall be blessed."

Here is the grand inclusiveness of God: "all the families of the earth."

We can identify with the Old Testament notion of a "chosen people." The term suggests a kind of exclusivity: these, but not those; some, but not others. If Israel is God's chosen people, then the rest of the families of the world appear to be like the undrafted players at the conclusion of the NFL draft: unwanted leftovers.

Truthfully, the Old Testament people of God may have been guilty of operating with precisely that sort of worldview. However, the expressed intent of God—dating back to a time when the nation of Israel was just an improbable promise to a childless older couple—was that Abram would be a vessel of blessing to "all the families of the earth."

Abram no doubt plays a unique role in salvation history. Still, he remains an example to us, for God's expressed purpose for the followers of Christ is no less broad and sweeping than his purpose for Abram. "Go into all the world and proclaim the good news" (Mark 16:15), Jesus instructed his disciples. God still has his heart set on all the families of the earth, and he still employs human vessels to bless them.

Finally, our Old Testament passage features this marvelous conclusion: "So Abram went, as the LORD had told him." It is a magnificent statement, and it triggers our imaginations on two levels. First, imagine what other verbs might have followed this passage. In Abram's case, the verb is "went." What verb might have been used if you or I had been in Abram's shoes? *Asked. Hesitated. Complained.* That Abram "went" is a great tribute to Abram.

Finally, imagine that each episode in our lives was recorded by the biblical writer. The writer was able to conclude this incident in Abram's life by saying that Abram did "as the LORD had told him." Imagine what would be written about you at the end of an episode in your life, at the end of a day at work, or an evening with your spouse, or a gathering with a group of friends. What a testimony if each chapter in my life and yours were lived in accord with what God told us.

FATHER OF THE FAITHFUL
Romans 4:1-5, 13-17

We noted above that Abraham continues to be an example to us in our day. Likewise, the apostle Paul regarded Abraham as a worthy example for the people of his day. To be more specific, Paul highlights the example of Abraham's faith.

Paul quotes two specific passages from the Genesis account of Abraham's story (Genesis 15:6 in verse 3; Genesis 17:5 in verse 17), though neither comes from the Abram passage above.

When Genesis reports that Abram believed God and that the Lord counted it as righteousness (15:6), Paul sees anecdotal proof of justification by faith. The law of Moses was not introduced for several centuries after the time of Abraham, so Abraham's righteousness was clearly not a function of the Law. Similarly, Abraham was not circumcised until later (Genesis 17:24); so Paul reasons (Romans 4:9-11) that Abraham's righteousness did not come from circumcision. Rather, Abraham's righteousness was by faith: "He believed the LORD; and the LORD reckoned it to him as righteousness."

The doctrine of justification by faith is given new insight in our computerized age. Previously, "to justify" something had the same connotation as "to rationalize" something. By this definition, the gospel truth remained intact, that is, justification was seen as the effort to make something right that is not right; but the association was a negative one. A person who tries to justify his actions, or justify himself or herself, is seen as someone who is making excuses.

Now, however, with so much of our day-to-day writing having moved from typewriters to computers, we have a new image to help us understand the doctrine. As you and I click away on a computer keyboard, we have constantly before us the option of "justified" type, which is a line of print that, by itself, would not reach the right margin. With one click, however, that line of type can be justified. What would naturally fall short is instantly put right.

In our sinfulness, we naturally fall short of God's glory (Romans 3:23), so we need somehow to be "put right" with him. That justification, Paul argues, is not by our own doing; it is God's doing, and it is by his grace.

In contending that justification is by faith and not by works, Paul distinguishes between "wages" and "gift." It is a distinction he returns to in 6:23: "The wages of sin is death, but the free gift of God is eternal life in Christ Jesus our Lord." "Wages," he observes, are what a person earns by his or her work. Wages are due to the worker, but God does not owe us salvation. It is the free gift of his grace.

To whom is this free gift given? Paul says that the promise is "guaranteed to all [Abraham's] descendants." At first hearing, that sounds exclusive; but, as we are discovering, God's offer is an open invitation.

As a category, the descendants of Abraham are important in Scripture. It is a significant claim that people make about themselves (John 8:33; Romans 11:1; 2 Corinthians 11:22). John the Baptist, however, seeing that peo-

ple regarded it as an important claim, questioned the intrinsic value of being children of Abraham apart from a godly way of living (Luke 3:8). Paul, too, expands the definition of what it means to be a descendant of Abraham.

In our passage from Romans, Paul divides the descendants of Abraham into two categories: "the adherents of the law" and "those who share the faith of Abraham." In other words, Paul is moving beyond a strict genealogical classification to a spiritual one. He makes the point still more bluntly to the Galatians, saying, "Those who believe are the descendants of Abraham" (3:7).

My wife and I have three young children. When each was born, people in our church made their assessments about which parent the baby favored. In the case of our middle daughter, people were especially struck by how much she resembled me. Several people said to me, "There's no mistaking whose daughter that is!"

Paul is making the same claim about believers. For Paul, the most prominent feature of Abraham was his faith. Faith, therefore, becomes the distinguishing characteristic, the family trait. If you have faith, the apostle Paul might nudge father Abraham, point to you, and say, "There's no mistaking whose child that is!"

In our Genesis passage, we noted that God's purpose for Abraham was inclusive rather than exclusive. God did not choose

Abraham and his family to the exclusion of the rest of the world but as a means of reaching and blessing the rest of the world. Indeed, Paul might say that God's will is not only for the whole world to be blessed by Abraham's descendants but for the whole world to become Abraham's descendants. It is an open invitation.

God's free gift is offered to all, and it is accessible to all. If genealogy determined the recipients, then most of the world would be left out. If circumcision, adherence to the Old Testament law, or works were the key, then most of us would be left out, too. However, the gift is not accessed by lineage or by law; the gift is accessed by faith.

In our next passage, Jesus calls to mind an Old Testament event that gives us a glimpse of how God's gift is accessed by faith.

R.S.V.P.
John 3:1-17

John introduces us to Nicodemus by noting three facts about him: (1) he was a Pharisee; (2) he was a leader of the Jews; and (3) he came to Jesus by night. None of these are understood as good things in the larger context of John's Gospel.

The fourth Gospel does not contain the expressed criticisms and warnings by Jesus about the Pharisees that we find in Matthew

16:5-12 or Luke 11:37-44. As the Gospel unfolds, however, the Pharisees are consistently portrayed as opponents of Jesus. They try to arrange for his arrest (John 7:32), they boast that they do not believe in him (7:48), they seek to undermine him and his works (9:13-34; 11:45-57); and they dispatch the soldiers that arrest Jesus in the garden (18:3). The fact that Nicodemus is identified here as a Pharisee, therefore, puts him in bad company in the Fourth Gospel.

Similarly, John's Gospel paints an unfavorable portrait of "the Jews." The issue should not be misunderstood as an ethnic prejudice, for Jesus, his disciples, and the Gospel writer himself were all Jews. However, when the Gospel refers to "the Jews" as a group, it is typically a generic reference to Jesus' opponents. The phrase "the Jews" appears over 60 times in John's Gospel. A dozen or so references are neutral or favorable. The great majority of references, however, are unfavorable. Therefore, Nicodemus's role as a leader of "the Jews" is not a flattering association in this Gospel.

That Nicodemus is perhaps regarded as a representative of the Pharisees, the Jews, or both is seen in verses 11 and 12. Jesus says to him, "Very truly, I tell you." "You" is singular in the original Greek. The other second-person verbs in these verses ("receive" and "believe"), however, are in the plural. When Jesus says to Nicodemus, "You do not receive our testimony" or "You do not believe," he is not speaking exclusively to Nicodemus. The verbs are plural, which suggests that Jesus is addressing a larger group, even though there is no indication that anyone else is there. Jesus is speaking to Nicodemus, but he is addressing all the Pharisees and the Jews Nicodemus represents, the ones who do not receive or believe.

Finally, the fact that Nicodemus came to Jesus "by night" is generally regarded as an indictment of Nicodemus. The "by night" detail is not an insignificant matter for the narrator, for when Nicodemus later assists in the burial of Jesus, he is identified as the one "who had at first come to Jesus by night" (John 19:39). The Gospel writer evidently believed that the timing of when Nicodemus came to Jesus said something about Nicodemus.

In the light/dark dualism of the fourth Gospel, coming "by night" can hardly be interpreted as a good thing. Night, Jesus says, is when people stumble (John 11:10); and as Judas abruptly hurries out of the Last Supper scene, the Gospel writer ominously observes that "it was night" (John 13:30).

Nicodemus's coming by night may represent his fearfulness, unwilling to be seen with Jesus in broad daylight. Fear of the Jews is identified as a motivating factor for others in John's Gospel (7:13; 19:38; 20:19).

Or Nicodemus's night may reflect the darkness and need of his soul. Two different times in the Gospel, Jesus says that he saves people from walking or living in darkness (8:12; 12:46). That Nicodemus came to Jesus in the darkness, therefore, may represent his need for "the light of the world" (8:12).

Finally, Nicodemus's night may symbolize his confusion. Confusion is certainly the hallmark of Nicodemus in this famous dialogue with Jesus. A chapter later, Jesus has a one-on-one discussion with an unlikely companion, a Samaritan woman. She seems able to engage in a sweeping and meaningful dialogue with Jesus, and their conversation by the well had ripple effects throughout her community. Nicodemus, this "teacher of Israel," however, seems unable to keep up with what Jesus is saying to him. He is all questions, and he does not grasp Jesus' answers.

In the end, Nicodemus's departure from the scene goes unnoted by the narrator. He fades back into the night from which he came.

While Nicodemus does not contribute much to the dialogue in John 3 besides bewilderment, we are indebted to him for what he elicits from Jesus. First, this is the conversation when Jesus introduces the concept of being "born from above." The more familiar phrase, provided by the King James translation, is "born again." The Greek adverb used here can mean either "again" or "from above." It appears two times in this passage (3:3, 7) in reference to the new birth. It is also used three other times in John's Gospel (3:31; 19:11, 23). In each of these instances, the phrase clearly means "from above." The translators of the NRSV, therefore, are on solid ground when they opt for "from above" in this passage.

Our understanding of the new birth is usefully informed by the images of both translations. Just as we were born physically (perhaps the meaning of Jesus' reference to being born "of water"), so we need also to be born spiritually—to be "born again." Just as our first birth is an earthly transaction, so the new birth comes "from above." (Many interpret the phrase "born of water" to be a reference to water baptism. Jesus' reference to being "born of water," however, follows in response to Nicodemus's question, "Can one enter a second time into the mother's womb and be born?" It may be, therefore, that the "water" refers to the womb, just as a child is born when the water breaks.)

Just as flesh gives birth to flesh, Jesus observes, so the Spirit gives birth to spirit. He uses a play on words to illustrate the working of the Spirit. "The wind blows where it chooses," Jesus says. "So it is with everyone who is born of the Spirit."

The word-play is not apparent in English; but in New Testament Greek (as in Old Testament Hebrew), the word for "spirit" and "wind" is the same. Jesus applied the attributes of the wind—"you hear the sound of it, but you do not know where it comes from or where it goes"—to those born of the Spirit.

If this is the nature of the Spirit, then perhaps it is incumbent upon the man or woman of God to be willing to be carried along by the Wind, though not knowing where he or she may be carried. Abram, in our Old Testament passage, proved himself to be easily and willingly driven by God's wind. Nicodemus, by contrast, never seemed to get off the ground.

Jesus chided him, saying, "Are you a teacher of Israel, and yet you do not understand these things?" Nicodemus is clearly in the dark. To the degree that Israel is dependent on its teachers, then by extension Israel, too, must be in the dark. Since Nicodemus was not able to understand the things Jesus was saying to him, Jesus turned to material that would surely have been familiar to Nicodemus: a story from Israel's history, taken from the Book of Numbers (21:4-9).

At one point in ancient Israel's journey through the wilderness, a plague of serpents infiltrated the camp. The people who had been bitten by the snakes were dying, and the people cried out for help. God's prescribed cure was a strange one: Moses should fashion a bronze serpent, hang it on a pole in the midst of the camp, "and everyone who is bitten shall look at it and live" (Numbers 21:8).

I wonder what hopes the first-century people of Israel cherished for the Messiah. Perhaps he would deliver the people from their oppression, like Moses. Perhaps he would lead the people in improbable victory, like Joshua. Surely he would reign in strength and justice, like David.

Who would have hoped that the Messiah would be like a metal snake? Who would have hoped that the long-awaited Messiah would be the image of an affliction, hung on a pole? Who would have conceived him as a Savior on a cross?

Surely we follow and worship one who delivers, one who wins, and one who reigns; but during this season of Lent, we are reminded that we also follow and worship one who took on the image of our affliction and hung on a pole. All who are afflicted and dying are invited to look at the one who hung on the cross and live.

In the passage from Romans, Paul teaches the central importance of faith. Faith is essential for our salvation. That truth is demonstrated in the story of the serpent on the pole.

The remedy for the snake-bit Israelites was not within themselves. Resolve and willpower were not going to get the job done. Neither was their cure found in some work or deed. They did not even

have to leave their tents in order to be healed, nor did they have to pay for or earn the remedy. All they had to do was look at the serpent on the pole.

That seems like a simple thing. Who would not do it? Well, I imagine the skeptic would not do it, because it sounds so implausible. I suspect that the person busily searching for a medication to buy would not take the time to do it. I suppose the person who was trying to save himself—frantically biting and spitting—would not look up to do it.

The Bible does not say one way or the other, but I would not be at all surprised if some Israelites died from the snakebites even after the serpent was erected on the pole. To be healed required looking at the bronze serpent; looking at the bronze serpent required a certain quality of faith.

Faith is our response to the salvation God offers us. While God's salvation is freely offered to all, not all respond. So it may be said that the gospel comes, like an invitation in the mail, with an R. S. V. P. at the bottom. Please respond!

Whether some were healed or all were healed in the wilderness, the opportunity was available for everyone. It was an open invitation. So, too, with the Son of Man, who "must be lifted up, so that whoever believes in him may have eternal life."

In the King James Version, God's open invitation was expressed in the word "whosoever." James

Edwin McConnell took that invitation personally.

McConnell was a well-known American church musician and religious radio personality in the first half of the 20th century. He put God's open invitation to music and gleefully sang, "'Whosoever' surely meaneth me, surely meaneth me, O surely meaneth me; 'Whosoever' surely meaneth me, 'Whosoever' meaneth me."

McConnell knew that God's open invitation had *his* name on it, and he rejoiced.

"Whosoever" also means you. Please respond.

Of We Only Knew

Scriptures for Lent:
The Third Sunday
Exodus 17:1-7
Romans 5:1-11
John 4:5-42

On stage or screen, this is the stuff of comedy. Two characters are in contact with each other, but one character does not realize that the other character is a future mother-in-law, a new boss, or some such. Only later, after the character speaks carelessly or behaves foolishly, does he or she discover, with much embarrassment, the actual identity of the other person.

The audience knows all along with whom the character is dealing, and we laugh as we watch the character make a fool of himself or herself. Later, when we see the character blush to recognize his error, we laugh at him again. Later still, as he awkwardly tries to get out of the self-inflicted difficulty, we laugh yet again. It is usually the stuff of comedy. Occasionally, however, it is the stuff of tragedy.

The most famous instance of this ancient plotline is the story of Oedipus. Having been abandoned at birth, Oedipus did not know his parents. The audience watches with horror as he unknowingly kills his father and marries his mother. He did not know with whom he was dealing.

Likewise, in Scripture, it is a tragic pattern that is played out again and again. People are in contact or conversation with God, but they do not realize with whom they are dealing. If it all works out in the end, it can be a little amusing. (For example, what Cleopas said to Jesus on the road to Emmaus in Luke 24:18.) Mostly, however, it turns out to be the stuff of tragedy.

Not knowing with whom they were dealing is the tragic error of those who ask, "Lord, when was it that we saw you ... and did not take care of you?" (Matthew 25:41-46). Likewise, it was poignant when Jesus prayed on the cross for the mocking mob, "Father, forgive them; for they do not know what they are doing" (Luke 23:34).

In our three passages for this week, we will see people who did not seem to recognize the God with whom they were in contact. We will see others come to the joyous realization of whom they were dealing with.

THE PEOPLE WHO DID NOT SEEM TO KNOW
Exodus 17:1-7

Exodus 17 begins with a statement that might be the summary of every Christian's spiritual pilgrimage: "From the wilderness of Sin the whole congregation of the Israelites journeyed by stages, as the LORD commanded."

The name of the wilderness from which the Israelites were emerging is pure coincidence. Elsewhere it is called the "Wilderness of Zin" (Numbers 20:1; 27:14). Its name in Moses' day did not carry the same meaning that the anglicized version of it does for us today. Still, the image of sin as a wilderness is apt, as is the picture of God's people leaving it rather than dwelling in it.

The use of the word *congregation* is important, for it reminds us of what Israel really was and was meant to be. They went down to Egypt as a large family, but emerged 400 years later as a small nation. The label accorded them here does not reflect size so much as function, however.

The original Hebrew word *adah* did not have the almost exclusively religious connotation that *congre-*

gation has for us today. Nevertheless, when the scholars created the Septuagint (the Greek translation of the Old Testament), the Greek word they used was *sunagoge,* from which of course we get *synagogue.*

In the Greek and English translations, we are given an image of Israel that goes beyond a large group of nomads or a multitude of freed slaves. They are, first and foremost, a gathering of God's people.

The congregation, according to Exodus, "journeyed by stages." That, too, provides a meaningful and helpful picture for us. Israel's journey was not a sprint. It was not a short trip that they could accomplish in one enthusiastic burst. Neither is our spiritual pilgrimage. Israel's journey and ours is accomplished in stages. We do not arrive all at once; we make our progress in phases.

The Lenten season is a good occasion for us to reflect on our spiritual journey. As you look back over your life, what stages do you see? They may not have been apparent at the time; but they become evident to us in retrospect, as the Lord faithfully, gradually leads us along.

It is noteworthy that this journey-by-stages was God's will for Israel: "as the Lord commanded." Evidently, it was not only God's will that they arrive at the Promised Land, it was also specifically his will that they travel there.

No doubt if God had wanted them to go from Egypt to Canaan instantaneously, he could have achieved it. That would have been no more miraculous than a number of other things God did in the process of delivering them from their bondage (Exodus 10:21-23; 14:19-31). Divine transport is certainly not unheard of in Scripture (Acts 8:39-40); but God did not choose to instantly convey Israel from origin to destination. Instead, he had them journey by stages.

I spent more than a decade in youth ministry. During those years, I led my youth groups on a lot of trips. We went on mission trips, performing tours, work projects, Christian festivals, and even two Holy Land tours. I discovered in the process that the journey was almost as important as the destination. Traveling together was an essential part of the group experience; those kids look back on the miles they traveled together in vans, buses, and planes with as much fondness as they do the actual place or event to which we were traveling.

So, too, with the ancient Israelites. God could have moved them instantly from Egypt to Canaan. In some respects, it might actually have been easier for him to do it that way than to endure the complaining and doubting ordeal of the Israelites in the wilderness. However, God wanted the people to make the trip, to make it together, and to do it by stages.

Likewise for us as Christians, the Lord intends for us to make our spiritual journey together, as part of a larger congregation and to do it gradually, steadily, by stages.

Along the way, the congregation of Israel came to a spot where "there was no water for the people to drink"; and this resulted in a great hullabaloo. The basic problem was that "the people thirsted there for water." That is a legitimate physical need. Not all our responses to our physical needs, however, are equally legitimate. We are sometimes preoccupied with our physical appetites. We may let them take priority over other more important matters in our lives (Genesis 25:29-34). We may attempt to satisfy them in ways that are inappropriate according to God's laws.

In this case, the Israelites' legitimate physical need became an occasion for quarreling, complaining, and faithlessness. Whatever the need—or the urgency of the need—the Israelites' response was an unhealthy one. Rather than complaining to Moses (Exodus 17:2-3) or doubting God (verse 7), imagine how peaceful and lovely it could have been if only the Israelites had made it a matter of prayer. Joseph Scriven might have been thinking of Israel in the wilderness when he wrote, "O what peace we often forfeit, O what needless pain we bear, all because we do not carry everything to God in prayer."

Moses did carry the matter to God in prayer. God answered the prayer and met the need.

The conclusion to the episode offers an insight not mentioned earlier: "The Israelites quarreled and tested the LORD, saying, 'Is the LORD among us or not?'" (verse 7). We do not find the people's remarks summarized like that in the preceding verses, but they are very telling remarks.

First, it is illustrative of the human preoccupation with things physical that the absence of water should make the people question the presence of God. The perpetual pillar (13:21-22) was not proof enough for the people, neither were all the evidences of God's provident care from when the Nile River bled to when the Red Sea parted. No, they were thirsty; and so they wondered what happened to God.

Our physical needs are perhaps the most severe challenges to our faith. "Skin for skin," Satan declared as it challenged God about the genuineness of Job's faith and faithfulness (Job 2:4). Knock over my body and there is a good chance that you will upset my soul. It is essential for us as Christians, therefore, to hear and to embrace the teachings of Scripture that invite us beyond the things of the flesh to the things of the Spirit.

Second, the murmurings of the thirsty Israelites prove that they did not fully recognize the God with whom they were dealing. That seems remarkable after all that they had seen and experienced, yet still their reflex was more to fuss than to trust.

At what point in our experience with God should we reasonably have it figured out? The fretting people in this passage were the same people who had been eyewitnesses to the plagues and the Passover. Not three months prior to this episode, the people had watched as God created a spectacular buffer to protect them from their enemies, made a way through the water for them, lured their enemies into a trap, and then in a moment delivered them and destroyed their oppressors. How could they, so soon after, doubt their God?

The Israelites are not alone. In Mark 6, we read the account of Jesus feeding a crowd of more than 5,000 with only five loaves of bread and two fish. Yet, just two chapters later, having seven loaves of bread and faced with a crowd of 4,000, the disciples worried aloud, "How can one feed these people with bread here in the desert?" (Mark 8:4).

You might think that the Israelites at Rephidim had seen and experienced enough to know the God they were dealing with. You might think that the disciples in Mark 8 had witnessed enough to know the Lord they were dealing with. The questions for us to consider are these: What do we know about God from what we have seen and experienced? To what extent do we live and believe accordingly?

HOW HE DEALS WITH US
Romans 5:1-11

Gamblers and investors are always hunting for a sure thing. The apostle Paul had found it.

Our selected passage from Romans 5 pulsates with Paul's confidence and certainty. Three times in eleven verses he references those things in which we can boast. Twice he uses the emphatic phrase "much more surely." Two other times he emphasizes his statements of certainty with the expressions "not only that" and "more than that."

The issue here is not self-confidence, however (although one suspects that Paul had his fair share of that). Paul had set aside confidence in himself and in law, lineage, and human wisdom in favor of complete confidence in the love, grace, and salvation of God. Those things of God so inspired Paul that he was confident even in the face of suffering.

Paul presents us with a strange genealogy—call it Suffering's Family Tree—as he traces the line that leads from suffering to hope. The connection may be a surprising one to us because typically we do not associate the experience of suffering with the feeling of hope. Quite the contrary. Our working assumption is that suffering leads to despair, not to hope.

Perhaps that is because much of what we call hope does not have a pure pedigree. Hope, for many of us, is indistinguishable from wishful thinking; it is "feeling encouraged." We feel encouraged, for instance, when circumstances show signs of improvement, when "things are looking up," as they say. It is after the team has won a few games in a row that the fans begin to feel hopeful. It is after the doctor reports good response to treatment that the patient dares to feel hopeful. Our hope, then, is descended from positive circumstances; it is not the result of godly assurance.

For Paul, however, hope is the offspring of suffering. The apostle has credibility on this point, for he was well-acquainted with suffering (2 Corinthians 11:23b-29).

The first generation of suffering, according to Paul, is endurance. We prove that truth in how we train people for certain occupations. Training camp for professional athletes and boot camp for soldiers are deliberately difficult experiences. Manufactured suffering is designed into the training specifically to build in endurance in the participants in the form of mental toughness and physical durability.

The offspring of endurance, Paul observes, is character. Character is the handsome grandchild of suffering.

When I was in junior high, I had an afternoon paper route. At times, when the weather was particularly unpleasant, I would try to convince my mom to drive me in the car on the route. She would tell me to go ahead and walk it, saying, "It will build character." Needless to say, I did not appreciate her answer. I am also sure, however, that her answer was correct.

The person who has not endured has opted instead for self-indulgence or quitting or pampering. Consequently, he or she has not developed character; he or she has settled for soft, spoiled, or selfish.

Finally, Paul concludes that hope is the progeny of character that is born of endurance and descended from suffering. The Greek word translated "character" here is used elsewhere by Paul to mean "ordeal" (2 Corinthians 8:2), "testing" (2 Corinthians 9:13), "proof" (2 Corinthians 13:3), and "worth" (Philippians 2:22). Such character is no pretense or façade. It is not put on in the morning with makeup. Rather, character is a weathered veteran. It is time-tested and proven. Itself a product of past experience, character gives birth to hope, which is a positive expectation for the future.

Paul's genealogy from suffering to hope stands in stark contrast to the behavior of the Israelites in the Exodus passage. Neither their suffering (that is, their thirst and need for water at Rephidim) nor their many past experiences with God's providence produced in them the kind of character that gave birth to hope. Rather than facing each challenge with hope, their instinct was to react to them in despair (Exodus 14:11-12, 17:3; Numbers 14:1-3).

We might say, in keeping with our theme this week, that the difference between Paul and the Israelites in the wilderness is that Paul recognized the God he was dealing with. Paul illustrates that by declaring how God dealt with him and how God deals with us.

Paul describes our beginning state with four words: "weak," "ungodly," "sinners," "enemies." Those words reflect our condition and our relationship to God apart from his gracious salvation. The great indicator of the kind of God we are dealing with lies in the fact that "Christ died for us" even while we were still in our helpless and wicked state. Our salvation is the initiative of God's love and grace. It is precisely that fact—that our salvation is rooted in God's nature rather than in our past, present, or future merit—that makes salvation a sure thing.

The new condition that follows in the wake of God's great salvation is marked by the words *justified, saved,* and *reconciled.* That is the beauty of how God deals with us. We were sinners, but he justifies us. We were due to suffer his wrath, but he saves us. We were his enemies, but he reconciles us to himself. "Amazing grace!"

You and I are free to proceed on our faith journey with confidence and certainty. Confident of our salvation. Confident in our status before God. Confident in the God we are dealing with.

THE PROCESS OF DISCOVERY
John 4:5-42

In John 3, we read of the encounter between Nicodemus

and Jesus. It is a great passage, to be sure; but Nicodemus himself is a disappointment.

Now, in the next chapter, we find the story of an entirely different kind of encounter with Jesus. It seems less promising at first. One might naturally expect a better result from a teacher of Israel than from this woman—a Samaritan woman, at that—who is traditionally understood to be living in sin. In the end, however, it is the woman, not Nicodemus, who discovers with whom she is dealing and responds with affirmation and joy.

In contrast to Nicodemus's nighttime visit, Jesus' conversation with the Samaritan woman occurred in broad daylight. While Nicodemus exited the earlier episode without mention and without effect, the Samaritan woman was decisive and fruitful.

Jesus initiated the conversation, asking the woman for a drink of water. To us, the request seems innocuous enough, but the woman recognized it as a surprising gesture given the Jews' calculated avoidance of Samaritans. She expressed her surprise that this Jewish man should ask her for a drink. Jesus responded, "If you knew the gift of God, and who it is that is saying to you, 'Give me a drink,' you would have asked him, and he would have given you living water" (verse 10).

This kind of take-it-to-the-next-level approach is typical of Jesus' conversations in the Gospel of John. In the synoptic Gospels (Matthew, Mark, and Luke), Jesus' parables make use of ordinary things to illustrate spiritual truths. In John, the stories we traditionally identify as the parables of Jesus are not quoted; but still Jesus uses the ordinary and the daily to signify and reveal something deeper, usually about himself. Thus, the appetite for bread leads to the revelation that Jesus is the bread of life (John 6:25-35). The healing of a blind man prompts a teaching about spiritual blindness (John 9). Here, in John 4, a water-cooler conversation becomes the occasion to reveal that Jesus is the one who offers living water able to quench thirsty souls.

It is noteworthy how quickly the conversation at the well turns from what Jesus requests to what Jesus offers. I suspect that is the standard experience of any who follow him. He invites us to live out our service to him in utterly human ways, in acts of charity, like offering a cup of cold water (Matthew 10:42; 25:35.). In the end, however, we find that the service we offer is eclipsed by the larger, longer-lasting gifts that he offers us (Luke 18:28-30).

Jesus turned the conversation from his request to his offer with this statement: "If you knew the gift of God, and who it is that is saying to you ..." Therein lies the crux of the matter: If only she knew. If she had only known who it was who was talking to her. She did not know (not yet, at least) with whom she was dealing.

What if she had? What if the Samaritan woman had realized with whom she was dealing? Jesus said that if she had known, she "would have asked ... and he would have given ..."

It is a classic conditional statement: If this, then that. I wonder, though, how you or I might have concluded the statement. If the woman had known, then she would have ... what? Worshiped? followed? converted? No, she would have asked. Jesus said that if the woman had known who he was, she would have asked for something. Perhaps, if the Israelites in the wilderness had fully recognized the God with whom they were dealing, they would have asked for their needs to be met rather than complaining, quarreling, and doubting.

Recognizing and asking is something of a natural pattern. When a famous person is recognized in a restaurant or airport, crowds ask for autographs or pictures. When a non-profit organization identifies who the money-people are in the community, that organization asks for those individuals' support. When a passenger on a plane realizes she is sitting next to an expert—a medical doctor, a psychiatrist, a financial planner—she asks for answers or advice.

This is how we operate. When we realize with whom we are dealing, we ask for something. What we ask for is a reflection on the person with whom we are dealing.

Accordingly, if we recognized with whom we are dealing when we are talking to the Lord, we would ask for things: big, eternal, life-giving, and truly satisfying things.

In the next few verses, the Samaritan woman displayed two common mistakes.

First, she underestimated Jesus. She looked at the well and the bucketless man. She looked at what she could see and understand; and she asked, "Are you greater than our ancestor Jacob?" She had no idea.

The second mistake the woman made was that she continued to think at the merely physical level, which in turn underestimated what Jesus had to offer. Told of marvelous "living water," which promised to thoroughly quench and to gush up to eternal life, the woman thought it would be nice to forego the chore of having to frequent the well to fetch water.

The woman's error is a familiar one. As physical creatures, we are inclined to think that the greatest things God could do for us are physical things—bodily healing, material blessings, or physical relief.

Suddenly, Jesus pushed the conversation forward again. First, he moved the dialogue from well water to living water. Then he moved the woman's limited recognition of what she needed to a deeper recognition. "Go, call your husband," Jesus told her, "and come back."

The woman responded by saying

that she had no husband, which was the truth but not the whole truth. Jesus demonstrated that he knew the whole truth, saying that she had had five husbands and was presently living with a man who was not her husband.

The woman's next move looks like a standard human reflex. Like a chess player who endeavors to maneuver out of danger, the Samaritan woman tried to redirect a conversation that had hit too close to home. Just when the exchange turned personal, the woman shifted it to the theoretical.

"I see that you are a prophet," she said. Then acting as if she were glad for the chance to pick a prophet's brain, she asked a rather academic question about the difference between where the Jews and Samaritans worshiped. Jesus minimized the distinction of place, turning attention to the more important issue: "to worship the Father in spirit and truth." Once again, the human preoccupation with an essentially physical issue ("on this mountain" or "in Jerusalem") is eclipsed by the more significant spiritual issue.

The woman did not seem to grasp the meaning of Jesus' words, so she conceded that the Messiah would one day "proclaim all things to us." Later in the Gospel (John 11:23-26), Martha postpones the hope of her brother's resurrection until "the last day," only to discover that she was in the presence of "the resurrection and the life." Likewise, here, the woman at the well is resigned to having all things clarified when the Messiah comes, only to be told that she is talking with him.

Perhaps, it was at that moment that the woman recognized with whom she was dealing. At first, she only saw Jesus as a Jew (verse 9). Later, she wondered if he were something more than an ordinary man (verse 12). Eventually, she recognized him as a prophet (verse 19). Finally, she ran back into town, wondering aloud if perhaps he were the Messiah (verse 29).

The Gospel reports that many of the Samaritans in that town believed in Jesus because of the woman's testimony (verse 39). They went out to meet him for themselves and invited him to stay with them. That the Samaritans extended such hospitality to a Jew was remarkable, as was Jesus' acceptance of it. John reports that many more came to believe in him "because of his word."

In the end, we are given a lovely portrait of how people come to faith in Christ: first, through the testimony of someone who has met him; then, subsequently, through a personal encounter with him and with his word.

The Israelites in the wilderness should have known the God they were dealing with, but they seem to have forgotten. The Samaritan woman did not know at first, but she—and eventually her whole town—came to know the truth. Similarly, Paul enjoyed the lively confidence of knowing, for he knew how God had dealt with him.

On stage or screen, a character who does not fully recognize with whom he or she is dealing is usually the stuff of comedy. For us, it is tragedy not to know or to forget the God we are dealing with.

In what area of your life are you forfeiting peace because you are not taking it to the Lord in prayer?

Jesus told the woman that, if she knew who he was, she would ask for something more. What more might you ask of Christ?

A Closer Look

Scriptures for Lent:
The Fourth Sunday
1 Samuel 16:1-13
Ephesians 5:8-14
John 9:1-41

The pastor sat on the floor of the sanctuary with the children of the church gathered around him. He pulled out of a bag two wrapped presents. One was large, colorful, and attractively wrapped with ribbons and bows. The other was small, dull, sloppily wrapped, and without adornment. The pastor held both presents before the boy next to him and said, "You can have either one. Which one do you want?"

As expected, the wide-eyed boy selected the large and pretty package.

The pastor queried several of the other children: "Is that what you would choose, too?"

The group was unanimous. They were most eager to see what was in the large and pretty package.

The big, fancy package turned out, of course, to contain a very small and modest gift—rather disappointing when compared to the packaging. When the pastor unwrapped the smaller, duller package for the children, however, they discovered a more expensive and exciting gift inside.

It seems that no matter how often we have heard, or said, that you cannot judge a book by its cover, we remain devoted to attractive covers. God and his word, however, challenge us to take a closer look.

In the selected passage from First Samuel, the prophet Samuel is encouraged to take a closer look when he is swayed by the outward appearance of Jesse's oldest son. In Ephesians, Paul reminds the Christians in Ephesus about when and how everything is seen clearly. In the story from the Gospel of John, "seeing" and "blindness" are redefined.

A LOOK INSIDE
1 Samuel 16:1-13

Israel looks on its throne and sees Saul. He is tall and handsome, and he has just returned from victory in battle. However, the Lord looks on Israel's throne and sees disappointment and disobedience. While the eyes of the people gaze on Saul, the eyes of the Lord turn to an overlooked field outside the little hill town of Bethlehem in the land of Judah.

For a generation, Samuel had been God's man and God's mouthpiece in the nation of Israel. He led the people himself for years; he was the one who anointed their next leader—their first king—Saul, son of Kish, from the tribe of Benjamin.

Saul, however, had not been careful to obey the Lord, so God told Samuel to find a replacement for Saul. While the pitcher is still on the mound, the manager has made a call to the bullpen. The bullpen was in Bethlehem, where Samuel was supposed to anoint one of the sons of Jesse to be the next king of Israel.

Interestingly, Samuel was afraid to follow the Lord's instructions. "How can I go?" Samuel asked God. "If Saul hears of it, he will kill me."

Samuel's response may surprise us, for he does not show any signs of fearfulness or timidity in the preceding chapters. Indeed, immediately prior to this passage, Samuel rebuked King Saul to his face, rejected Saul's pleadings, and personally killed and cut into pieces the captured Amalekite king, Agag. Samuel was no shrinking violet.

Many people find confrontation difficult, even frightening; but Samuel fearlessly told truth to power. At the beginning of Chapter 16, however, the same prophet who had been unafraid to confront King Saul to his face was frightened to do something behind his back.

Of course, we and all our relationships would be healthier if we had Samuel's balance. Families, friendships, workplaces, and churches would all enjoy more wholesome dynamics if people were unafraid to go face-to-face but reluctant to go behind a back.

Samuel's fear of Saul's reaction, we discover, was a reasonable one. In the chapters that follow, we see Saul respond with violent paranoia when he suspects that his son Jonathan (1 Samuel 20:24-33) and the priests at Nob (22:11-19) are conspiring against him behind his back. Saul had made numerous attempts to capture and kill David.

Saul had not shown any such brutal outbursts prior to this point in the story; but perhaps Samuel sensed in him the growing mental, emotional, and spiritual turmoil. Saul was becoming an unpredictable and volatile man, and Samuel was afraid to cross him.

You and I may take comfort in the fears of the saints. Time and again in the pages of Scripture, we see great men of God react to divine assignments with fear and reluctance (Moses in Exodus 3:1-4, 17; Gideon in Judges 6:11-15; Jeremiah in Jeremiah 1:4-8; Simon Peter in Luke 5:4-10). We are reassured to see that these people, who were mighty instruments in God's hand, were made of the same frail stuff we are.

At the same time that we are reassured by their reluctance, however, we may also be challenged by their obedience. While they were not greatly used by God because of their innate courage, they were greatly used by God simply because they allowed themselves to be used by him. They obeyed. Here in 1 Samuel 16, Samuel obeyed.

The specific guidance from God was that Samuel would find the next king among the sons of Jesse of Bethlehem. When the first of those sons, Eliab, was presented to Samuel, he looked at him and thought, *Surely the Lord's anointed is now before the Lord.*

It is an interesting anachronism that Samuel identified Eliab as "the Lord's anointed." Anointing someone was precisely what Samuel was sent there to do, but he had not yet. It probably reflects the Old Testament understanding that "the Lord's anointed" was equated with "the Lord's chosen." Even before anyone had been anointed that day, Samuel thought of Eliab as the Lord's anointed simply because he assumed that Eliab was the one whom the Lord had chosen.

Eliab, it turned out, was not the one whom the Lord had chosen. Samuel was making an assumption based on outward appearances.

Samuel's humanness is familiar to us. He saw Eliab, and he had seen enough. The things that are visible are, naturally, the first things we see. They form our first impressions. They influence our judgment. Samuel's first reflex on this occasion was a superficial one.

It is ironic that Samuel was taken with Eliab's "appearance" and "the height of his stature." When we are first introduced to Saul in the biblical narrative, we read, "There was not a man among the people of Israel more handsome than he; he stood head and shoulders above everyone else" (1 Samuel 9:2b). Saul was a tall, good-looking man; yet his reign became a tragedy. Still, when presented with the tall and handsome Eliab, Samuel assumed that he was the Lord's man for the job.

Since Samuel was one of the great men of God in the Bible, we know that an instinctive response to things external is not limited to the ungodly. And, since Samuel lived 3,000 years ago, we know that superficiality was not invented by our contemporary culture.

Still, our contemporary culture pays particular attention to things superficial. We have made presentation an art and packaging a science. Products are endorsed less and less by experts and more and more by beauties. A popular singer's looks seem to be as important as the quality of his or her voice. Physical attractiveness has even become a prerequisite for those who broadcast news.

Of course, beauty and sparkle should not be dismissed as evil things. Before Madison Avenue and Hollywood learned how to surround us with beautiful images, the Creator had already done it. As Cecil Alexander wrote, "All things bright and beautiful ... the Lord God made them all."

Eliab's physical beauty was no more a liability than it was a qualification. We later discover that David, whom the Lord did choose and whom Samuel did anoint, was also physically attractive (1 Samuel 16:12). The point is that, for God, physical appearance is irrelevant.

As Samuel stood ready to anoint the attractive candidate, Eliab, God corrected him: "The LORD does not see as mortals see; they look on the outward appearance, but the Lord looks on the heart."

God certainly has us pegged. We do "look on outward appearance"; but the great revelation in this passage is what God says about himself: "The LORD looks on the heart."

Perhaps we are embarrassed when our outward appearance is unsatisfactory: when an outfit is unflattering, when the necktie has a stain, when there are blemishes on our faces, or when it is a bad hair day. Most of us do what we can to look our best before we go into the world each day. Probably each of us has had an occasion when we have thought or said, "I just don't want anyone to see me!"

What would it be like, though, if we were turned inside out? What if the hair and the clothes that we spend time and money on were

not visible to anyone? Would we continue to invest anything in them? What if, instead, the content of our hearts were open for all to see?

I remember hearing a gentleman in a church some years ago bemoan the fact that one Sunday morning a young usher was wearing tennis shoes. "Don't you think God is bothered by that kind of disrespect?" he asked me.

I do not know about the tennis shoes. I do suspect, though, that if God looks on the heart, there are more disturbing things than tennis shoes in most churches on most Sundays.

We would be mortified to find, at the end of the day, that we went through the day with a piece of food visibly stuck between our two front teeth. How much more terrible, at the end of the day, to discover that we have been carrying around bitterness or a grudge stuck in our hearts or to have prejudice, greed, or lust marring our appearance before God?

The season of Lent has traditionally been used by Christians for spiritual reflection and introspection. While the world around us may be preoccupied with what is on the outside, we might use this season to consider what is on the inside, what is in our hearts.

The Bible does not tell us what was in Eliab's heart, or in David's, for that matter. What we can learn about those men from this passage is not as important as what we discover about God. We discover that the Lord looks on the heart—on Eliab's heart, on my heart, and on your heart.

One by one, the sons of Jesse were presented to Samuel; and one by one, Samuel had to ask for the next. When Samuel reached what appeared to be the end of the line without the Lord having chosen any of the seven sons presented by Jesse, Samuel asked, "Are all your sons here?"

No. There was still the youngest—a boy named David, who was out with the sheep.

Was it that the shepherding task was perceived to be too important, and so David was not available with the rest of the family? Or was it that the youngest of eight was perceived to be so unimportant that he was an afterthought, an oversight?

If young David was forgotten and overlooked that day, it was the last time. He rose quickly to national prominence in Israel and eventually to the throne. God promised him an everlasting dynasty (2 Samuel 7:16). Later biblical historians ranked subsequent kings by comparing them to David (1 Kings 15:1-3, 11). A thousand years later, the birth of Christ occurred in "the city of David" (Luke 2:11). Over 30 years later, when Jesus entered Jerusalem, the crowd's hopeful greeting was to "the son of David" (Matthew 21:9). Today, David ranks as one of the great heroes of the Bible, as well as one of the most famous people in ancient world history. He has been immortalized in paintings, statues, and stained glass. Three thousand years after he lived and died, his star still flies on the flag of the modern state of Israel.

At Samuel's word, David was brought in from the fields. As the young shepherd boy stood before the old prophet, the Lord said to Samuel, "Rise and anoint him; for this is the one." He was the one, indeed.

A LOOK IN THE DARK
Ephesians 5:8-14

I have three young children: a baby, a preschooler, and a third-grader. I see in each of them a rather innocent relationship to darkness.

I notice that both the preschooler and the third-grader are uneasy in the dark. Being afraid of the dark, in varying degrees, seems to come with the territory of childhood. Children always want nightlights. Even as adults, we find ourselves in unnerving situations that remind us that we are not naturally nocturnal creatures.

Our baby, meanwhile, shows no signs of being afraid of the dark. Then again, a baby shows no signs of being afraid of anything. She can be startled, to be sure, and in that sense frightened; but fear in the sense of dread is a later development. Fear requires more knowledge than a baby has, and so my baby is not afraid of the dark.

My three children are all young enough to have innocent relationships to darkness. What is so perverse about fallen humanity, however, is not that we are afraid of the dark but that we are afraid of the light.

At its best, darkness is peaceful, romantic, or restful. On the other hand, darkness can be menacing and frightening. We are unsure of ourselves in the dark, because we cannot see. Scripture tells us that, at its worst, darkness provides some people ease precisely because they and their works cannot be seen (Luke 22:53; John 3:19; Ephesians 5:12-13).

Darkness is where we can be comfortable in our shame. Comfort is appealing, to be sure; but we ought not become comfortable with some things. Darkness lends privacy to what we do not want anyone to know about or see. In this passage, we sense that the apostle Paul wants to come in, pull up the shades, and let the light pour in.

The biblical story, you recall, begins in darkness. Darkness and chaos set the stage for the beginning of the Creation story, and God's first creation was light (Genesis 1:2-3).

The start of the Creation story, then, becomes the pattern for the gospel and a metaphor for our individual experience with Christ. God shines his light into darkness: the darkness of a lost world and the darkness of an individual life (Matthew 4:16; John 1:4-5; 8:12; 2 Corinthians 4:4-6; 1 Peter 2:9). That is the premise with which Paul begins in our passage from Ephesians.

The striking thing about Paul's initial statement is the absence of prepositions. He does not say of the Ephesian Christians that they were once *in* darkness but rather that they *were* darkness. Likewise, their present reality in the Lord is not that they are *in* the light but rather that they *are* light.

So it is that Paul exhorts the people to "live as children of the light." The offspring imagery Paul employs is helpful, for it suggests that light is our heritage and our home. As children of God, light should be our native land and language. Light is where you and I ought to be most comfortable; light is what we ought to bring to the world around us. We are children of the light, and Paul says that we ought to live accordingly.

As we look inward during this Lenten season, we do well to consider in what areas of life we have chosen to keep the shades drawn.

Where and how do we choose to live in darkness? Where and how do we need to open up and let God's light shine in?

THE POWER TO SEE
John 9:1-41

If I were asked to find my way from one part of town to another without being able to see, I would find that extremely difficult. I would need the help of others.

I would travel slowly and uncertainly. I would probably hurt myself along the way. I would possibly get lost.

Jesus sent the man born blind to wash in the pool of Siloam. The blind man had to find his way there, to another part of town, without being able to see, without the benefit of a seeing-eye dog, and without Braille letters on directional signs along the way. Yet, there is no indication in the story—not even a hint—that the man had any trouble with the trip. In fact, it is reported in a straightforward way that "he went and washed and came back able to see."

I do not doubt the blind man's acquired ability to find his way around, to be independent, and to take care of himself. I marvel at it, but I do not doubt it. What strikes me in the story is that the blind man is the only character (apart from Jesus) who is not manifestly groping, bewildered, confused, or lost.

The blind man apparently did not need to ask anyone any questions in order to get from here to there, but everyone else in the story is full of questions. In just this one episode, eleven different questions are asked by characters other than the blind man and Jesus. Likewise, the blind man does not show any uncertainty in his journey; but everyone else in the story is abuzz with uncertainty.

The pattern of questions and confusion begins right at the outset. The disciples see this man, who had been born blind; and they ask Jesus a theological question: Was his blindness the result of his sin or his parents' sin?

Old Testament theology featured a certain cause-and-effect paradigm for life. It is not monolithic in the Old Testament, but it is a prominent theme (perhaps best exemplified in Deuteronomy and Proverbs). The basic belief was that wise and obedient living yields blessing, while foolish and sinful living brings pain and difficulty.

The problem with the disciples' question to Jesus is that it reflected a little reverse logic. Namely, if sinful living results in difficulty for a person, then it must follow that difficulty in a person's life indicates sinful living. (This is the same logic Job's friends used in their not-so-helpful conversations with their suffering friend.) According to the disciples' logic, this man's blindness must be traced back to sin. There was no question about that. The only question was, Whose sin? Was it the sin of the blind man himself or his parents?

Jesus disputed the disciples' basic premise, saying that the man's blindness was not the product of sin. In our modern sensibility, we welcome that word; but then Jesus offers a different viewpoint. "He was born blind so that God's works might be revealed in him."

The explanation of the man's blindness remains a theological one, and that may surprise us. The issue, it seems, is not past product but future purpose. The blindness was not a product of human fault or weakness; the blindness was for the purpose of God's strong work.

Then Jesus spat on the ground in order to make a little mud, which he spread on the blind man's eyes. Jesus' strange method of healing is unexplained in he text. We see him healing elsewhere by touch and by word; however, this messy and humiliating approach seems unnecessary. On the other hand, if we have a need that Jesus is willing and able to meet, what method would we decline?

In the days of the Old Testament prophet Elisha, Naaman, a proud military man from Syria, came looking to be healed of his leprosy (2 Kings 5). Elisha prescribed for Naaman seven baths in the Jordan River. The method did not appeal to Naaman. As a result, he almost missed the opportunity to be healed.

Perhaps, the blind man had heard along the way the story of Naaman. Perhaps he had thought to himself, "If I were in his shoes, if I were ever offered the chance to be healed, I would do whatever it took!" Here was his chance, so he found his way through the streets of Jerusalem, with mud on his face, in search of a pool where he could wash. He washed, and he saw.

From that point on, confusion about the man's identity pervades the story. Again and again, people are uncertain whether this sighted man is the same man as the one who had been born blind. Part of the uncertainty may be an indictment of the carelessness of the people involved. Perhaps this blind man was little more than fly-over country for the seeing population of Jerusalem. He was familiar only as an obstacle, a nuisance by the side of the road. Perhaps most of the people had never stopped to talk to him, to help him, to look at him; so when the time came, they found it hard to recognize him. The man's most prominent features for many indifferent passersby were his blindness and his begging posture. With that condition removed, they were unable to make a positive I.D.

Most of the uncertainty about the man's identity, however, was likely born out of disbelief; and it is a good illustration of how preconception can determine perception. The preconception at work in this case was that a person born blind could not possibly be given the power of sight. Therefore, since this particular man could see, he surely could not be the same man who was born blind.

Jonathan Swift wrote that there are none so blind as those who will not see. Such is the irony of the Pharisees' interrogations of the once-blind man. He was known for being blind but now could see quite clearly. The Pharisees, by contrast, had always had the power of sight; but they refused to see.

By the end of the story, the Gospel writer reveals that the central issue is not the once-blind man. He and his blindness are at the center of the controversy, to be sure; but they are not the issue.

The real confusion concerns not the identity of the blind man but the identity of Jesus. The real problem of blindness, it turns out, is not the physical blindness of the man who was healed but the spiritual blindness of the Pharisees and their companions.

The Pharisees were blind to who Jesus was. Apparently, they were determined not to see him for who and what he was. Our modern idiom says that a person is "in the dark" when they do not know or understand something. The Pharisees were "in the dark" about Jesus. They stand in stark contrast to the man who had lived his whole life in physical darkness but who ended up believing and worshiping (John 9:38). These men whose eyes had always been able to see light could not see the Light of the world (John 8:12) when he was right there in their midst.

Finally, we discover that the Pharisees were also unable to see themselves. Overhearing what Jesus said to the once-blind man about real sight and real blindness, some of the Pharisees protested, "Surely we are not blind, are we?" They perceived the figurative language Jesus was using (and which is typical of Jesus in the Gospel of John) and were challenging his implication.

Jesus, however, does not respond by debating the point with the Pharisees. He does not try to prove their spiritual blindness (which has become evident to the reader) nor does he force them to prove their sight. Instead, Jesus ends the conversation with this provocative statement: "If you were blind, you would not have sin. But now that you say, 'We see,' your sin remains."

How ironic that, at the outset, the blind man is perceived by the disciples to be sinful precisely because of his blindness. The Pharisees, too, are certain of his sinfulness (9:34). However, Jesus turns the tables. It is not those who are blind but those who claim to see who are saddled with sin.

We are encouraged in these passages of Scripture to take a closer look, to take a closer look within at our hearts, which is what truly matters. We are encouraged to take a closer look at our living, whether it reflects the light of Christ or "the unfruitful works of darkness." We are encouraged to take a closer look at Jesus, who calls us from darkness into light and who is himself the Light.

We have all been afraid of the dark at some time in our lives. When in your life have you been afraid of the light?

If someone looked on your outward appearance, how might he or she describe you? If someone could look on your heart, how might he or she describe you?

Coping With Death

Over the course of 20 years in ministry, I have witnessed death and people coping with death. I have sat with people in the hospital as they have died. I have met with grieving families, and I have officiated at many kinds of funeral and memorial services.

Individuals cope with death in different ways. I have seen people who are so coolly matter-of-fact that they seem completely undisturbed by death. I have seen others so torn up with grief that I have wondered if they would ever smile or laugh again. I have watched grieving family members show real discomfort with the body of the deceased loved one, while others need to touch and kiss and talk to the corpse. I have participated in services where there has been a continuous, audible sobbing; and I have been in other services that were marked by laughter and celebration. People cope with death in different ways.

Likewise, different cultures cope with death differently. The handling of the corpse, the rituals and rites that accompany death, the accepted expressions of grief, the methods of community response and support, and the beliefs about what happens after death—these all vary widely from one culture to another.

In the passages before us this week, we get a narrow glimpse of how different people in Scripture coped with death. The more significant matter, however, is that we see how God copes with death.

GOD AND EZEKIEL
IN DEATH VALLEY
Ezekiel 37:1-14

Many times I have driven along Skyline Drive in Virginia. Because the scenic road winds its way through the Blue Ridge Mountains, the traveler is greeted every few miles by breathtaking views of the valleys below. I have, on numerous occasions, stopped and gotten out of my car to enjoy the panoramic vistas: the graceful mountains, the uncountable trees, and the vibrant palette of nature's colors.

If you have stood and looked over a valley, you know the kind of glorious spectacle that fills both eyes and heart. Now imagine that splendid valley without the trees, the grass, the creeks, the flowers, and the wildlife. Imagine that valley, instead, covered with bones. Dry bones.

The Lord gave Ezekiel a sight to see, a panorama of death that had three noteworthy characteristics.

First, it was not a valley of skeletons; it was a valley of bones. The image is not just of death but of dismemberment and destruction. A skeleton, at least, is recognizable as a thing that was once alive. Scattered, detached bones, however, are the stuff of a wasteland.

Second, Ezekiel notes that "they were very dry." No medical examiner is required to set the time of death. It was a long, long time ago. In our day, the person whose heart has just stopped can, in some instances, be revived; but this vision is not a picture of "just died"; this is a picture of "long dead."

Finally, Ezekiel reports that the valley was full of these dry bones; there were "very many." This was not a little roadkill by the side of the highway. This was death in every direction as far as the eye could see, an uncountable number of unrecognizable casualties.

Ezekiel was set down in the midst of them. God did not give the prophet a detached view from a safe distance. Rather, Ezekiel was among them, as though he were himself one of them. He was surrounded.

Of course, Ezekiel was one of them, not one of the dead but one of the group that those dry bones represented. Namely he represented, "the whole house of Israel" (verse 11). They represented Ezekiel's people; he was one of them.

That the Lord set Ezekiel down in the midst of this terrifying vision—not on the outskirts overlooking the mess—is typical of God's call. Jeremiah, like Ezekiel, did not preach to a people at a distance. He lived among them and shared their fate. Likewise, Moses was not the one who had sinned, yet he spent 40 years in the wilderness with the faithless generation he was called to lead. It is typical of God's call in our lives that he asks us to do his work right in the midst of the valley. After all, that is what he himself did in Christ's incarnation: "The Word became flesh and lived among us" (John 1:14).

It was there in the middle of the valley that God asked Ezekiel the crucial question: "Mortal, can these bones live?"

God asked people a lot of questions in the pages of Scripture. He had questions for Adam and Eve (Genesis 3:8-13), for Cain (4:9), and for Abraham (18:13). He asked questions through the prophets (Jeremiah 2:5; Ezekiel 18:2, 31; Hosea 11:8). Jesus asked questions of both his followers (Matthew 16:13, 15) and his opponents (22:41-45).

At first, it seems unnatural that an omniscient God should ask questions of human beings. We quickly discover, however, that his questions are not those of a student but those of a teacher. He asks questions not because he needs to know the answers but because we need to know the answers. We need to say the answers.

So the Lord asked Ezekiel the question, the crucial question that Ezekiel needed to answer out loud: Can these bones live?

Coming from anyone else, of course, it would be a preposterous question. Can this game that ended two months ago still be won? Can this tree that was chopped down last year still bear fruit? Can the Titanic still reach its destination? Can these dry, dismantled bones still live? It is a ridiculous question.

Not only is the question ridiculous, but the Lord asks Ezekiel the question in the hardest place to answer it. When we stand at a distance, we may be able to see hope in a difficult situation. However, when we are right in the midst of it, surrounded by it, we find it hard to see anything but the present, inescapable reality.

Ezekiel answered, "O Lord GOD, you know."

In our soundbyte culture, we may be weary of hearing politicians give non-answers, hedging answers, and evasive answers. At first blush, Ezekiel's answer sounds like the non-committal kind. In reality, Ezekiel's answer is a great statement of faith. The prophet places the matter squarely where it belongs: with God.

Too often God's people have been guilty of knowing better. Sarah knew better than to think that she and Abraham could still produce a child (Genesis 18:10-12). The ten spies knew better than to think that the Israelites could defeat the Canaanites (Numbers 13:25-33). The mourners at Jairus's house knew better than to think that the dead girl needed only to be awakened (Luke 8:51-53). Give Ezekiel credit for not knowing better than to think that these bones could live.

You or I may be standing in the midst of some improbable situations, lost causes, or hopelessness. It may be that the Lord wants us to ask and answer the question: Can these bones live? Granted, the question may be ridiculous; but then the answer may be beautiful.

Next, God gave Ezekiel a pair of strange instructions. First, he was to prophesy to the bones. Then, he was to prophesy to the breath.

It is interesting that God did not instruct Ezekiel to stand back and watch. It certainly would have illustrated the point of what God can do if Ezekiel had been just a spectator watching the mass of bones rattle together and come to life. However, the episode reveals God's characteristic preference for involving his people in his work. Obviously, the miracle in the valley was entirely God's achievement; yet God chose to require Ezekiel's participation. Ezekiel could not do it by himself; God would not do it by himself.

The particular method of Ezekiel's participation is also characteristic of God's work. The Lord did not instruct Ezekiel to stoop down and begin a manual process of assembling the bones together into skeletons. Rather, the Lord instructed Ezekiel to prophesy to the bones.

The importance of the spoken word is revealed throughout Scripture. Proverbs (10:11, 19-21) and James (3:5-12) report the grand potential for goodness or wickedness in the spoken word. Jesus holds up the spoken word as the great barometer for what prevails in a human heart (Matthew 15:10-20). It stands to reason that ultimately we should be justified or condemned by our words (Matthew 12:36-37).

Beyond the importance and impact of human words, Scripture bears witness to the power and effect of God's word. When God speaks, things happen, from creation itself (Genesis 1:3) to healing (Luke 7:6-10) to miracles (Luke 8:24-25) to whatever he intends (Isaiah 55:10-11).

When God commands Ezekiel to prophesy, we are reminded of the power of the proclamation of God's word. For when Ezekiel prophesies, the dismembered bodies come back together. When Ezekiel prophesies again, those rebuilt bodies come to life.

It is worth noting that the Old Testament understanding of *prophecy* was larger than our common usage of the term. Our understanding of *prophecy* is limited almost entirely to "predicting." For us, to *prophesy* is to "foresee" and "foretell." In the Old Testament, however, *prophecy* included "predicting" but was not limited to predicting. The prophet proclaimed God's word, which may have been about the future or the present or even the past.

We do not know the content of what Ezekiel preached to the scattered bones or later to the air. We do know that Ezekiel obeyed the improbable instruction and that both bones and breath responded to God's word.

Once the deed is done, God offers Ezekiel an explanation of what he has just seen. The bones represented the whole house of Israel.

Israel had been pronounced dead—and, indeed, had been dismembered—long before. The twelve tribes of Israel had not been united under a single throne since the tenth century B.C. The northern tribes had long since been obliterated by the Assyrians, and now the southern tribes had been conquered and largely exiled. The "whole house of Israel," it seemed, was a lost cause.

We discover repeatedly in the pages of Scripture, however, that our God specializes in lost causes. Such is the nature of our great salvation. So here, in the valley of this vision, God promised that the dead and dismembered house of Israel would be reunited and resurrected. In spite of their wicked, disappointing past, God had a good future in store for them.

Finally, the language of God's promise to his people in Ezekiel's day continues to be meaningful to God's people today. "I am going to open your graves, and bring you up from your graves, O my people," God said. Five centuries before Christ, the prophet has spoken a conspicuously New Testament promise, which brings us to our other two passages for this week.

THE ESSENTIAL INGREDIENT
Romans 8:6-11

We read the ingredients on a simple candy bar, and we are surprised (and perhaps dismayed) to discover all that goes into a little sweet-tooth snack. Read the ingredients on a human being, meanwhile, and we are surprised to discover how basically simple our composition is.

In the Genesis account of creation, we are privy to the component parts of humanity. "The LORD God formed man from the dust of the ground," Genesis reports, "and breathed into his nostrils the breath of life; and the man became a living being" (2:7).

So it is that our list of ingredients is a short one: "dust of the ground" and "the breath of life." Dust and breath. No more, no less.

That brief list of ingredients in Genesis may translate into the spirit-and-flesh paradigm found in the New Testament. The flesh represents that dust-of-the-earth part of ourselves; the spirit represents what God breathed into us.

Jesus suggested those two categories to the disciples in Gethsemane. "The spirit indeed is willing, but the flesh is weak" (Matthew 26:41.) Paul observes the same two component parts of a human being in several places (1 Corinthians 5:5, 2 Corinthians 7:1; Colossians 2:5).

In Old Testament Hebrew and New Testament Greek, the words *spirit, wind,* and *breath* are used interchangeably. When Genesis reports that God breathed "the breath of life" into the man's nostrils, the Hebrew word translated "breath" also means "spirit." Similarly, in Ezekiel, when God instructs the prophet to "prophesy to the breath," the original Hebrew features another word that can be translated both "breath" and "spirit."

Meanwhile, on the cross, Jesus prayed, "Father, into your hands I commend my spirit" (Luke 23:46). Then he died.

It was at the moment when God breathed into the dust that "the man became a living being." Likewise, it was only after the "breath" entered the reassembled bones that "they lived, and stood on their feet." Conversely, it was when Jesus released his Spirit to the Father that he died. We conclude, therefore, that it is the Spirit that gives life to the flesh. Spirit is the essential ingredient.

It is against that larger backdrop that we can understand the beauty of what Paul means when he writes to the Romans, "To set the mind on the flesh is death, but to set the mind on the Spirit is life and peace." The Spirit gives life (John 6:63; 2 Corinthians 3:6).

In this brief passage, Paul uses a few prepositions to create a multitude of images. First, there is the matter of what one's mind is "set on": Spirit or flesh (Romans 8:6-7). Next, there is the question of what one is "in," again either the flesh or the Spirit (verse 8-9). Finally, there is the issue of whether or not Christ or the Spirit is "in" us (verses 10-11).

While there is not a continuity of images to create a single, integrated picture, there is an unmistakable theme: Spirit vs. flesh.

In the contemplativeness of this Lenten season, we are invited to ponder our relationship to the Spirit and our relationship to the flesh. The invitation goes beyond pondering: we are invited to set our minds on the Spirit, to live in the Spirit, and to have the Spirit live in us. That Spirit, we discover, leads to life. In the end, that

Spirit "will give life to your mortal bodies," just as the Spirit raised Jesus himself from the dead.

GOING TO THE TOMB
John 11:1-45

The cave-grave near Bethany was a quiet spot. The dead body of Lazarus had been buried there four days before. At this particular moment, there was no one else around. Jesus and his disciples had not yet arrived in Bethany. Mary and Martha, along with the many friends who had come to comfort them, were back at the house. So the tomb was a quiet place—just the sound of the breeze in the trees.

That quiet spot, however, is the center-stage for this story. The tomb is where Lazarus lay. The tomb is where Mary did not go. The tomb is where Jesus did go. The tomb is where Lazarus emerged from.

When the story opens, Lazarus is not yet in the tomb but is deathly ill. His sisters, Mary and Martha, have sent word to Jesus about Lazarus's condition. The three siblings were apparently friends of Jesus. They expected that their friend, who had healed so many others, would come and heal Lazarus.

Jesus received the message in time, but he did not come immediately. Instead, he tarried two more days in the place where he was with his disciples.

It seems like callous disregard on Jesus' part to receive an urgent plea and not respond with urgency. Imagine a 911 operator who did not answer the phone because she was on another line chatting with a friend. Imagine an ambulance driver who thought he would swing by the grocery store on the way to the emergency.

Many of us have, at times, felt that answers to our prayers were postponed by God. We do not understand why. All we know is that we called out with great exigency, but God did not seem to respond with corresponding urgency. We gather that Mary and Martha might have felt the same kind of surprise and disappointment about Jesus (John 11:21, 32), as did some of the bystanders (verse 37). So the issue for much of the passage revolves around what Jesus could have done; no one seemed to be giving much thought to what Jesus still could do. That may be our error, as well.

By the time Jesus did finally reach the area, Lazarus had been dead and buried for four days. When Martha heard that Jesus was arriving, she went to meet him, while Mary stayed in the house with those who had come to comfort.

Martha's greeting to Jesus is a marvelous mixture of grief and faith, and it leads to a seminal conversation with Jesus. Jesus assures Martha that Lazarus will rise again, and Martha affirms her belief that "he will rise again in the resurrection on the last day." That statement prompts Jesus to respond, "I am the resurrection and the life."

The Gospel of John is well-known for the great "I am" statements of Jesus (6:35; 8:12, 58; 10:9, 11; 14:6; 15:5). They reflect John's central concern for identifying who Jesus is. This passage contains one of the most familiar and significant of those statements: I am the resurrection and the life.

The contrast between what Martha says she believes and what Jesus says he is lies in two different understandings of "resurrection." For Martha (as well as for many folks today), the resurrection is regarded as an event; and that event was, in her mind, an eschatological one. According to Jesus, however, the resurrection is not an event, but a person. It is not found at a certain point in time but rather it is found in him at all times.

This is no small matter of semantics, for it raises the critical question of whether people are looking for resurrection and life in the wrong place and the wrong time. While many in our culture blithely walk around with a vague assumption about an afterlife, Jesus does not endorse Martha's "last day" scenario. He does not point to the future; he points to himself. Ultimately, our faith does not cling to a doctrine or a philosophy but to a person.

After her substantive dialogue with Jesus, Martha returned to the house where she told Mary that Jesus wanted to see her. At that, Mary got up and hurried to meet Jesus.

When they saw her hurry out of the house, the people who were there to comfort Mary assumed that "she was going to the tomb to weep there." That was a fair assumption, and it reflects a natural reaction: the instinct to go to the grave and grieve. In this particular instance, however, the assumption was incorrect. Mary did not go to the tomb; Mary went to Jesus.

I see a long line forming behind Mary. It is a line of believers that stretches through the ages, from first-century Bethany to our 21st-century world. Mary and Martha were among the first grieving believers to go to Jesus in their sorrow, and we have been doing it ever since. We do not turn to death but to the one who is the life. We do not slink off to despair; we run to hope. Our destination is not the grave; it is Jesus.

When Mary met Jesus, her greeting was the same as her sister's had been. Jesus did not have the same extended dialogue with Mary that he had with Martha, perhaps because they were not alone. Instead, moved by her weeping, Jesus asked where Lazarus's body had been laid. They answered, "Lord, come and see."

That invitation is a familiar one in the larger context of John's Gospel. It is Jesus' invitation to his first disciples (1:39). It is Philip's invitation to Nathanael (1:46). It is the Samaritan woman's invitation to her fellow townspeople (4:29).

Now that same invitation is extended to Jesus, but in a very different context. While the other instances are invitations for people to come to Jesus, this instance is an invitation for Jesus to come to a tomb. Such is the nature of what we have to offer him, what we invite him into and where we need him to come.

Then Jesus wept. It is a short statement that says a lot. Jesus seemed to know even before arriving what he would do when he got there (11:11); still he wept. His compassion was not preempted by his power. Even though he knew that he would bring Lazarus back to life, still he wept for those who were grieving Lazarus's death.

We are encouraged to trust God's wisdom and God's timing. Though a situation may be confusing, frightening, or even tragic for us, we are taught to trust God, to trust that he knows best, and to trust that he will work everything out in the end. That "big picture" trust might seem to put God at a distance from us, but Jesus' tears belie that distance. That the Lord is able to see more and do more than we are does not lessen his sympathy. That he can work things out in the end does not diminish his companionship, compassion, and care in the meantime.

So Jesus wept, probably just like those many others who had come to comfort Mary and Martha. Those others, however, could only stand and weep. Jesus wept, but he could do more. He told them to take away the stone.

It was a ghoulish prospect, and Martha's sensibilities were clearly horrified by it. While everyone else is gathered respectfully at the graveside, one friend of the family suddenly suggests that the coffin be dug up and pried open. It was a preposterous suggestion. As preposterous, perhaps, as the instruction to prophesy to a bunch of bones.

Martha worries aloud that there will be a great stench. Jesus responds, "Did I not tell you that if you believed, you would see the glory of God?"

Therein lies the great dichotomy between human reason and faith. Reason considers the implications of the stone being moved and fears the stench. Faith considers the implications of Jesus being the resurrection and the life and sees the glory of God.

After the stone was removed, Jesus prayed aloud and then cried out, "Lazarus, come out!"

As in the Ezekiel episode, the deed is done by words. There is no resuscitative action taken, no contact with the corpse. Jesus simply speaks, and the dead man comes to life. He speaks, and the mummy-like Lazarus emerges from the cave. "He speaks," wrote Charles Wesley, "and listening to his voice, new life the dead receive."

It is an astonishing picture of two men. One stands outside the tomb; the other lies dead within the tomb. The first calls to the second, and the second man comes out of the tomb alive. It is a picture of what happened one day near Bethany. It may also be a picture of what will happen one day all around the globe. For the apostle Paul says that, when Christ returns, it will be "with a cry of command" (1 Thessalonians 4:16). Paul does not say what that command will be; but perhaps it will be, "Come out," and "the dead in Christ will rise first."

Taken together, this week's passages give us a lovely glimpse into how our God copes with death. Namely, he conquers death and he offers life.

Our human aspiration is not so much to conquer death, for we are more realistic than that. Our best human efforts are merely to delay it. However, God demonstrates the marvelous capacity to conquer death, even after death has apparently already won. In Ezekiel's valley and Lazarus's tomb, the final score was already posted on the board. Nevertheless, the word of the Lord changed the final score—post facto, post mortem—and suddenly there was life where once there had been death.

Life is the real issue. Life, abundant and eternal, is what God has always wanted for humankind. From the beginning, he has been breathing his Spirit into us, for the Spirit gives life. Giving life is how God addresses death.

We noted in the story of the valley of dry bones that Ezekiel could not bring the bones to life by himself, and God would not bring them to life by himself. In what particular ways have you sensed that God has wanted to use you in his work? In what new ways do you suspect he might want to use you in his work?

To what extent is your mind set on the flesh? To what extent is your mind set on the Spirit?

The Same Mind

Scriptures for Lent: The Sixth Sunday
Isaiah 50:4-9
Philippians 2:5-11
Matthew 27:11-54

We use the word *mind* to explain a lot about ourselves and other people. When someone behaves irrationally, we conclude that he was "out of his mind." We critique what seems to us to be a foolish decision by saying, "She was not in her right mind." When we want to express our fear and frustration in the midst of difficult circumstances, we say that we felt as if we were "losing our minds." A prosecuting attorney will try to reveal the defendant's "state of mind" at the time of the crime.

The apostle Paul used the word *mind* to explain something about Jesus as well as something about the way you and I ought to be. "Let the same mind be in you," he wrote to the Philippians, "that was in Christ Jesus."

We have bumper stickers, buttons, and bracelets with the initials "W.W.J.D." reminding us always to ask, "What would Jesus do?" Paul invites us to go a layer deeper. The key to what Jesus did was his "mind." If we have the same mind, then we will live the same way.

Isaiah provides a portrait of that same mind. Written several hundred years B.C., the passage is not explicitly about Jesus. Many Christians have taken the passage to be a "messianic prophecy," however, and as such an insight into the person and work of Christ. In this case, the passage gives us a glimpse of the "mind" that Paul later commended as a model to us.

Finally, this week's Gospel passage features Matthew's account of Jesus on the cross. Here, in this most important of passages, we read the familiar story of what happened to Jesus from his appearance before Pilate to his death on the cross. Our particular focus for this week, however, is not on what was done to Jesus but on what Jesus did and how he did it. To the outside observer, Jesus may have appeared as "object" in the grammar of that Friday's events. We know better, however. We know that Jesus was "subject," not "object." So we examine what he did and how he did it.

A GLIMPSE OF HOW HE WOULD DO IT
Isaiah 50:4-9

The Ethiopian eunuch, reading from another section of Isaiah, asked Philip, "About whom, may I ask you, does the prophet say this, about himself or about someone else?" (Acts 8:34). That is a fair question to ask again and again throughout the books of the Old Testament prophets, including our selected passage from Isaiah 50.

The passage is written in the first-person singular. In the course of just a few verses, the verb tenses toggle between references to the past, the present, and the future. It requires an interpretive leap, therefore, to read this passage as descriptive of Jesus, who clearly did not write it and who was not even born until at least 500 years later.

That is precisely the leap we make, however, when we talk about *prophecy*, and especially so with *messianic prophecy*. We credit the text with insight beyond the borders of its own time. And, in the case of a text that is regarded as messianic, we presume that the text provides insight into Christ—his identity, his purpose, and his experiences.

The larger theme at work in this portion of Isaiah is the theme of the Lord's servant. The calling, work, characteristics, and experiences of that chosen servant are all referenced. Just who that servant is, however, is a question of interpretation, just as it was for the Ethiopian eunuch. The servant is, at times, explicitly identified as the nation of Israel (41:8; 44:1; 49:3). Elsewhere, the servant appears to be an individual (42:1-4; 52:13–53:12) and is explicitly not Israel in 49:5-6. Matthew understood the servant reference in Isaiah 42 to be fulfilled by Christ (Matthew 12:17-21). Likewise, Jesus took a statement similar to our passage and applied it to himself (Isaiah 61:1-2; Luke 4:16-21).

Our endeavor is to explore the mind that was in Christ Jesus. It is explained in Philippians and embodied in Matthew. Here, in Isaiah, we seek points of connection with the other two lections and with the mind of Christ.

The selected passage from Isaiah 50 resembles our two New Testament passages in three respects: (1) the attitude of the speaker is similar to the attitude attributed to Christ in Philippians; (2) the experience of the speaker brings to mind the experience of Christ's passion, a portion of which we have in the Matthew 27 passage; and (3) the speaker in Isaiah expresses confidence in ultimate victory, which is explicit in the Philippians passage and implicit in the Matthew passage.

We recognize a Christ-like sweetness, meekness, and purpose

in the Isaiah 50 speaker. That he has the tongue of a teacher, of course, is reminiscent of Jesus' earthly ministry. Beyond that, his words are specifically directed to "sustain the weary." That deliberate attention to those who are weak and needy is consistent with Jesus' stated sense of purpose (Matthew 9:11-13; 11:28-30; Luke 4:17-21; 19:10). It is an easy thing, tempting even, to concentrate attention on those who are healthy, whole, attractive, and important. This teacher, however, speaks to and for the weary.

The image of the speaker's relationship with God, too, is a lovely one, and again suggestive of Jesus. This one who teaches is first a listener and a learner. He is attentive to what the Lord says to him. Similarly, Jesus said, "I have not spoken on my own, but the Father who sent me has himself given me a commandment about what to say and what to speak.... What I speak, therefore, I speak just as the Father has told me" (John 12:49-50).

The most striking similarity to Christ, however, is in the suffering. The speaker's obedience in verse 5 seems to lead to his abuse in verse 6. Paul, likewise, wrote that Jesus was "obedient to the point of death" (Philippians 2:8). The specifics of the speaker's suffering (being struck on the back, insults, spitting) all bring to mind Christ's suffering before and on the cross. The speaker's attitude toward that suffering ("I gave my back to" and

"I did not hide my face from") are central characteristics of Christ's Passion. His participation is portrayed as willing, even voluntary, which we will explore further in our two New Testament passages.

Finally, there is in Isaiah 50 the hint of ultimate victory. The speaker, though abused, still has the confidence to speak challenging words to his would-be adversaries. He is certain of the Lord's vindication (verse 8), the Lord's help (verses 7 and 9), and his enemies' demise (verse 9). In like spirit, Paul's account of Jesus' humiliation (Philippians 2) concludes with Christ's exaltation. Similarly, even though the Matthew passage is principally about Jesus' suffering and death, it concludes with reports of certain triumphant events and even a testimony from some of his torturers.

Our chief concern is the mind that was in Christ Jesus. Isaiah 50 does not explicitly mention him; but it does offer prophetic insight into his purpose, attitude, and experience. The mind reflected by the speaker in Isaiah 50 surely seems to be the same mind that was in Christ Jesus.

REMEBERING HOW HE DID IT
Philippians 2:5-11

From time to time, one individual in an organization is commended to the rest of the group for his or her exemplary performance. For attitude or productivity, for sales or effectiveness, the prized performer is presented to the group as "an example to us all." The message is that, if every employee worked like this employee, if everyone on the team performed like this player, if every volunteer in the organization gave like this member, then we would truly become what we ought to be.

Such is the nature of Paul's message to the Christians in Philippi. Paul holds up before the group the incarnation, obedience, death, and exaltation of Christ and says, in effect, "He is an example to us all."

Interestingly, however, it is not specifically what Christ did that serves as an example for us. That is to say, we do not begin where Christ began ("in the form of God"); thus the path we are expected to follow is not exactly his path. Likewise, we are not expected to die an atoning death, nor to be raised to unparalleled and universal honor. Christ's role is unique; so we do not follow his example in the sense of being who he was or doing what he did.

Paul cites those specifics, however, as a way of illustrating the underlying matter, the matter that is an example to us all. "Let the same mind be in you," Paul wrote. That is the core issue here—not what Christ did but the mind that was in him that prompted him to do what he did.

The recurring, pivotal word in this passage is "form." It appears three times in our translation (although two different Greek words were used originally by Paul). Paul writes that Jesus was, prior to his incarnation, "in the form of God," that he then took "the form of a slave," and that he was "found in human form."

In the first two instances, Paul uses the same Greek word, *morphe,* and thus establishes a dramatic contrast. Originally, Jesus was in the *morphe* of God; but then he voluntarily took on the *morphe* of a slave. Because our English borrows from the Greek, we have the concept of "morphing"—to change the form, the appearance, or the character of a thing. In the case of Christ, that transformation represents a complete and unthinkable demotion.

Apart from history books, we have had no contact with slavery. The people to whom Paul wrote, however, knew all about slavery. They were surrounded by it. Indeed, some of the people who read Paul's letter were probably slaves themselves. For Paul and his audience, therefore, the word *slave* was not just picturesque or metaphorical language. *Slave* was close to home. *Slave* was a word that had up-close-and-personal meaning.

Slaves were not masters. Slaves were not sovereign. Slaves were not free. Rather, a slave was a person who was owned by someone else. A slave was under the authority of another. A slave was property at the disposal of his or her master. To suggest that someone would exchange the form of God for the form of a slave is so outlandish that it defies reason.

There is no adequate human analogy for what Christ did, but even an inadequate analogy gives us some sense of the descent. Imagine that the multimillionaire who owns both the sports team and the stadium forfeits his or her ownership and chooses instead to walk the aisles selling beer and peanuts. Imagine that the corporate CEO abandons his or her corner office and six-figure salary in favor of the mailroom. Imagine that the four-million-dollar-per-picture actor forsakes his or her starring roles to put makeup on other actors and actresses.

The starting height is not as great as Christ's nor the chosen depth as low, but the human analogies tell us that no one in his or her right mind would make those choices. Yet that is the mind, according to Paul, that should be in you and in me.

The counsel is not unique to Paul, of course. Jesus himself taught an approach to living and interacting that makes his followers seem to be out of their minds: To offer yourself vulnerably to the person who has just slapped you (Matthew 5:39), to actively love those who hate and mistreat you (Luke 6:27-28, 35), to forfeit great wealth in order to follow Jesus (Mark 10:21). The world looks and says, "No one in his right mind would make those choices."

That was the mind that was in Christ Jesus, however, and that is the mind that ought to be in us.

The step that comes between being in the form of God and taking on the form of a slave is an illustrative one. Paul said that Jesus "emptied himself."

The Greek word found here is used elsewhere by Paul to refer to something that has been made null (for example, Romans 4:14). Write "VOID" in big, bold letters across your check, and then see how much it is worth. This is the steep step Christ took: voluntarily jettisoning his worth and his status in favor of a manger and a cross.

In our vernacular, we speak of a person being "full of himself" when he is unbearably proud or manifestly preoccupied with his own interests. In contrast to the self-absorbed person who is full of himself, Christ emptied himself.

Christians have traditionally made the season of Lent a season of self-sacrifice. Many times, we observe the season by giving up something; an act that is for our own good (giving up caffeine or chocolate). What Christ gave up, however, was not for his good but for ours. Perhaps we might give some thought to what we may need to empty ourselves of for the sake of Christ or someone else, a sacrifice at our expense rather than to our benefit.

Paul continues. Just when we think we have reached the basement, the apostle opens a door and shows us yet another flight down: "Being found in human form, he humbled himself." Christ had already made the move from the form of God to the form of a slave, yet he went down still further. He humbled himself.

The word Paul uses for "humbled" appears almost a dozen times in the New Testament. Perhaps the most picturesque usage comes from John the Baptist, when he says, "Every valley shall be filled, and every mountain and hill shall be made low" (Luke 3:5). The imagery here is of the landscape being leveled off, low places filled in and high places smoothed over. As a result, the hills and mountains will no longer be recognizable. They will amount to nothing. The word for what will happen to those mountains and hills is the same word Paul used to describe what Jesus did to himself. What Jesus did to himself he did with a particular destination in mind.

On one trip to Israel, our tour group visited a medieval church that had been erected to commemorate a sacred spot. The entryway to the church was conspicuously small, and one of our members asked the tour guide why. He explained that it was made smaller during a time of combat so that invading armies could not ride into the church on their horses or even come running in quickly. Through that small entrance, you could only come in slowly, carefully, and crouched.

I had to crouch down to enter that old church. My destination required a certain posture. Likewise, Jesus' destination required a certain posture. He had to humble himself to the point of obedience; and a severe obedience at that, for it was "to the point of death." His destination was not merely the form of a slave; his destination was the cross. To get there, he had to be made low.

There is something almost ghoulish about Paul's counsel here. He points to the example of a person who meekly subjected himself to an unjust death sentence and a cruel execution; and then he says, "That's it! Be like that. Think like him."

The standard operating procedure in the worlds of business or sports is to imitate success. We interview the player, the coach, the executive who has made it to the top of his field; and then we imitate what he did. By contrast, Paul points to the one who seems to have chosen the down escalator, commending that example to us for emulation. To be sure, Christ was exalted in the end; but that reflects what God did for him not what he did for himself. What Christ did for himself —to himself—was twofold: He emptied himself (verse 7), and he humbled himself (verse 8). That reveals the mind that was in him, and Paul urges you and me to have the same mind in us.

We have noted Jesus' model of servitude. This is a part of how we are instructed to be like him. What in you resists being a servant? In what way or in what place should you perhaps take on "the form of a slave"?

HOW HE DID IT
Matthew 27:11-54

The scene opens with Jesus on trial. It is, of course, one of the great preposterous scenes in Scripture. Beautifully preposterous just as the Christmas tableau or the sight of Jesus washing his disciples' feet is. That the immortal God should become a baby or that the king of the universe should be crouched down in servitude borders on absurdity. Likewise, that the one who will judge all the nations of the earth should himself stand trial with puny mortal fingers pointing at him and an inconsequential human potentate passing sentence on him seems nonsense.

It is not nonsense, however. It is grace. Because grace is undeserved, grace by definition cuts across the grain of logic. Logic says here is how it should be, only to have grace come along and say, yes, but here is how it is going to be. Logic says that the prodigal should be punished; grace says that he will be embraced. Logic calls for a lost and rebellious humanity to be abandoned to the consequences of their insubordination; grace seeks and saves the lost. Logic says that the sinner should be damned; grace wants the sinner to be saved.

So we rejoice in the preposterous picture: Jesus, at whose very name "every knee should bend," in human custody; God's grace at the mercy of a human judge.

This is precisely the kind of submission foreshadowed by Isaiah and promoted by Paul. We should note that Christ's suffering here does not qualify as oppression, inasmuch as oppression is generally imposed by a stronger other. Submission, by contrast, is a voluntary yielding to another. Being oppressed is not my choice; submitting is my choice. I may be mistreated in both instances, but my mind and my participation are not the same in both instances. Here, as we saw in the Isaiah and Philippians passages, the mind that was in Christ Jesus was submissive.

Matthew reports that "the governor was greatly amazed" when Jesus did not answer any of the charges made against him. Pilate apparently recognized that Jesus was innocent and that the Jewish leaders did not so much have a case against him as a plot against him. It may be that Pilate did not want to do what, in the end, he felt forced to do. Perhaps, therefore, Pilate hoped that Jesus would put on a defense so that he could judge in Jesus' favor. At the very least, Pilate surely expected Jesus to put on a defense, for he was an innocent man who was facing the prospect of cruel torture and a gruesome death.

The Monday morning quarterback sees so clearly what the player, the team, and the coach should have done. He watches a player fail at what appears to be a routine play, and he cries out with indignation at his television set. He articulates his frustration and bewilderment in a question: "Why didn't he just ...?" followed by whatever easy and obvious thing the player failed to do.

We are bewildered when we see someone fail to do something that seems to us easy and obvious. Pilate was bewildered, for it must have seemed to him an easy and obvious thing that Jesus could have done. With just a little effort at defending himself, with just a little testimony on his own behalf, Jesus could have poked holes in the weak and inconsistent case of his accusers. Why didn't Jesus do the easy and obvious thing to escape? Pilate had no idea.

Pilate had no idea how easy it would have been for Jesus to escape. Jesus had already shown uncanny, perhaps supernatural, ability to elude those who wanted to kill him (Luke 4:28-30; John 8:59; 10:39). Beyond that, Jesus assured his followers that he could, with a word, be rescued by a dozen legions like none those human soldiers had ever seen before (Matthew 26:53).

Moreover, Pilate had no idea that Jesus did not aspire to escape. The instinct to preserve and protect our lives seems universal. Yet, Jesus did not show any of our natural self-preservation reflexes. He did not contend with his accusers, he did not defend himself, he did not resist his torturers, and he did not plead with the judge. In short, he did nothing to stop the unjust execution that was being orchestrated by his opponents.

Here, as we mentioned earlier, is where Jesus is subject rather than object. Here we see "the mind that was in Christ Jesus."

If Jesus had been the unwilling victim of those who conspired against him—if he had gone kicking and screaming to the cross—then he might be reckoned the object of unfair and abusive treatment. However, Jesus went quietly and willingly to the cross. Pilate and his wife resisted the turn of events more than Jesus himself did. We remember that Jesus said, "I lay down my life in order to take it up again. No one takes it from me, but I lay it down of my own accord. I have power to lay it down, and I have power to take it up again" (John 10:17-18).

He did take it up again, of course, on Easter Sunday. So the humiliation is not the end; death and defeat do not have the final word.

As we noted earlier, the Isaiah passage ends with confidence, and Paul's word to the Philippians concludes with Christ's exaltation. Here in Matthew, even before the Easter Sunday account, we see several ripples of victory in the wake of Christ's death: (1) the opening up of human access to God, as symbolized by the tearing of the Temple curtain (verse 51); (2) the defeat of death, as symbolized by the opened graves and raised bodies (verses 52-53); and (3) the testimony of the centurion and his companions. Christ, who had taken the form of a slave and was thus unrecognizable as God, in this moment on the cross, was recognized: "Truly this man was God's Son!" (verse 54).

"Savior on a Cross" is our theme for this Lenten study; and here is the passage, more than any other, where we see it. In Matthew 27, we see the Savior on a cross. We see him tortured and bleeding. We see him mocked and taunted. We see him misrepresented and misunderstood. He has been humbled, indeed. Made low, indeed.

Through it all, what was he like? He did not retaliate. If he had, that sneering, spitting mob would not have known what hit them. He neither attacked others nor defended himself. He did not seek rescue or revenge.

Paul says, "Let the same mind be in you."

You and I are not called on to do the things that belong uniquely to the person and work of Christ. But we are called on to live our lives in the same way, with the same mind.

I do not expect that you or I will have to face cruel, public execution. I am quite sure, however, that you and I will be misrepresented and misunderstood from time to

time. I am certain that we will encounter unfair treatment and unkind talk. When we do, then what? Then let the same mind be in us that was in Christ Jesus.

You and I do not need to die for the sins of others. We do need at times, however, to take on the form of a slave. We will be in situations where we might like to retaliate. We will have plenty of opportunities to humble ourselves, to empty ourselves, and to be obedient. So we are challenged to have the same mind that was in Christ Jesus.

When we are treated unfairly or unkindly; when we need to have an attitude of servitude; when our reflex is to attack or to retaliate; when we are inclined to pursue our own interests rather than obeying God or serving others; or when we are just plain full of ourselves, he is an example to us all.

No everyday situation in our lives is comparable to Christ's experience on the cross, but in what everyday situations in your life might you be more Christ-like? By humbling yourself? by keeping silent? by self-sacrifice?

We are not inclined to voluntarily submit, especially when it leads to our mistreatment. In what relationships or circumstances do we need to voluntarily submit?

In what ways is the mind that was in Christ Jesus different from the mind that is in you?

Happy Beginning

Scriptures for Easter:
Acts 10:34-43
Colossians 3:1-4
Matthew 28:1-10

From childhood, we are acquainted with happy endings. The people in the story may go through terrible difficulties, but in the end they come out all right. The obstacles are overcome, the difficulties resolved, the villain defeated, and the protagonists vindicated.

In the fairy-tale versions of a happy ending, there is not much story left after the resolution. We do not see the routine married life between Cinderella and Prince Charming. We do not follow Sleeping Beauty after her kiss. What happens after the climactic resolution is summarized with the phrase "and they lived happily ever after."

The Gospels boast a happy ending, to be sure; but it is not a fairy-tale ending. Matthew, Mark, Luke, and John could have ended their accounts with the great climax and victory of Easter. They could have featured in the final scene a gleaming and glorious risen Lord. The curtain could close on that triumphant sight with the nar-rator's voiceover declaring, "And he lived happily ever after."

None of the Gospel writers made that choice, however. Matthew, Mark, Luke, and John knew better than to make the Easter event the happy ending to their accounts, for it was not the end. Rather, it was the happy beginning.

Three of the writers—Matthew, Mark, and John—added a little more to their reports after the story of the Resurrection. The fourth, Luke, added a great deal more to his report, writing an entire second volume (the Book of Acts) to follow up what happened after the Resurrection.

A fairytale ending leads us to believe that the conflict and the climax are the only things worth detailing. Everything that happens afterward can be blurred together under the broad heading of "happily ever after."

The ending to the Gospel story is not so vague. What follows is quite specific. You and I are to follow him on this side of the empty tomb.

GOOD NEWS FOR EVERYONE
Acts 10:34-43

Good news is rarely universal. I watch the sports scores tick across the bottom of the screen, and the same score that makes me smile makes another group of fans scowl. The rain forecast that pleases the farmer displeases the picnicker. So it is that good news for one person is almost always bad news for another person. Not so with the gospel. Here is good news for everyone.

Peter and the early church were slow to recognize this truth. Although Jesus' instructions seem clear to us in retrospect (Matthew 28:19-20; Acts 1:8), the early church continued to function with an old reflex.

The first followers of Jesus were all Jewish, as Jesus himself was. Since the Jews understood themselves to be the chosen people of God and the Christians recognized Jesus as the promised Jewish Messiah, many early believers found the concept of a Gentile Christian incomprehensible. Some dismissed the idea altogether. Others assumed that a Gentile would have to become a Jew before becoming a Christian.

Furthermore, the Jews of first-century Palestine were encouraged to embrace a kind of exclusivity. They were to maintain a distance from Gentiles in order to preserve their purity. Surrounded by pagans, they clung to a belief that God had a plan and purpose exclusively for them.

This exclusivity was reflected and reinforced by the floor plan of the Temple. Separated at the center was the Holy of Holies where God was particularly present. Nearest to God in the Temple layout were the priests, then the Jewish men, and then the Jewish women. Finally, on the outskirts of the Temple was the Court of the Gentiles.

God-fearing Gentiles were welcome to come and pay their enlightened allegiance to the God of Abraham, Isaac, and Jacob. However, even there in common faith, they were not permitted to stand on common ground with the Jews who were, symbolically, closer to God.

One God-fearing Gentile was a Roman officer named Cornelius, who was stationed in Caesarea. Caesarea, the Roman headquarters in Palestine, was located on the western coast, along the Mediterranean Sea. Peter was in Joppa, 35 miles to the south, staying with Simon the tanner. An angel appeared to Cornelius and told him to send for Peter.

The next day, Peter went up to the roof of the house where he was staying. Hungry and in prayer, Peter had a vision.

Peter saw a large sheet let down from heaven, and the sheet was full of unclean animals. The Old

Testament law had spelled out a strict dietary code for the Jews (Leviticus 11), which Peter carefully observed. He recognized immediately that the animals presented to him were not permissible to eat, yet he heard a voice instructing him to kill and eat. He protested to the Lord that he never had eaten anything unclean; but the voice replied, "What God has made clean, you must not call profane" (Acts 10:15).

This back-and-forth between Peter and God occurred three times. The message in triplicate is reminiscent of Jesus' conversation with Peter in John 21:15-19, and perhaps that familiar repetition assured Peter that this was from the Lord.

Peter was left alone on the roof to ponder the meaning of what he had seen and heard. Meanwhile, there was a knock at the door downstairs. It was messengers from Cornelius, inviting Peter to come to Cornelius's house.

Two days later, Jewish Peter stood in the home of Gentile Cornelius. After hearing Cornelius report what the Lord had communicated to him, Peter spoke to Cornelius and those assembled in his house. Peter's speech is recorded in our passage from Acts.

Peter's message was about Jesus, what he had witnessed with Jesus, and the salvation offered in Christ. Peter began his speech, though, with what he had only recently come to understand: "God shows no partiality, but in every nation anyone who fears him and does what is right is acceptable to him" (verses 34-35).

The statement is astonishing. In some circles, it would have qualified as heresy. Peter finally recognized the breadth of God's good will and the scope of Christ's salvation. The gospel that Peter preached was good news for everyone.

This sample of Peter's preaching offers an embryonic glimpse of the four Gospels. Matthew, Mark, Luke, and John did not write the story of Jesus' life, ministry, death, and resurrection until years after his ascension. The early church was preaching the gospel long before the Gospels were written. This example of Peter's preaching suggests that the written Gospels were expanded versions of what the church was already proclaiming: John's baptism, Jesus "doing good and healing," his death, his resurrection, and his instruction to testify about him.

On this Easter Sunday, we are especially interested in what Peter has to say about Christ's resurrection. We may note, perhaps with some surprise, the deliberate limitations of Christ's appearances after his resurrection. Peter said that "God allowed him to appear" to a select group of "witnesses," but "not to all the people."

Jesus' ministry leading up to the cross had been very public. While there was a select group of disciples around him, his teaching and his miracles were not limited to that inner circle. Now, however, after the Resurrection, it seems that God did not allow Jesus to appear publicly but only to the chosen witnesses.

Peter does not offer an explanation of the policy, but it may be that Jesus did earlier. In Jesus' story of the rich man and Lazarus (Luke 16:19-31), both men die and go to their rewards. Lazarus is comforted, while the rich man is tormented. From his place of misery, the rich man asks a favor of Abraham: "Send (Lazarus) to my father's house—for I have five brothers—that he may warn them, so that they will not also come into this place of torment.... If someone goes to them from the dead, they will repent" (verses 27-28, 30). Abraham replies, "If they do not listen to Moses and the prophets, neither will they be convinced even if someone rises from the dead" (verse 31).

Those concluding words would only have been a dramatic statement when Jesus first spoke them. After he rose from the dead, however, they took on new meaning. People would not be persuaded by the Resurrection, but by testimony and Scripture. Moses and the prophets had borne witness before; now a new, contemporary group was "chosen by God as witnesses." Peter was among those witnesses; now he bore witness to Cornelius and a houseful of Gentiles.

The specific testimony about Jesus is summarized by Peter in two phrases. First, "he is the one ordained by God as judge of the living and the dead" (verse 42). Second, "everyone who believes in him receives forgiveness of sins through his name" (verse 43).

It is the will of God (that all would come to repentance) that animated the early church. They lived under a standing order: "to preach to the people and to testify." Thus the resurrection of Christ is not a happy ending but a happy beginning, for the mission of the church had just begun.

Finally, Peter's conclusion is an interesting one: "All the prophets testify about him." The prophets to whom Peter referred are the Old Testament prophets. At a minimum, he was referring to those men for whom 16 of the final 17 books of our Old Testament are named. Peter may have been thinking even more broadly than that.

There are many other individuals in the Old Testament who are identified as prophets but who do not have books named for them (Nathan and Elijah). Furthermore, a handful of books that we think of as history books (Joshua, Judges, First and Second Samuel, First and Second Kings) are identified by the Jews as "former prophets." David, too, was recognized by Peter as a prophet (Acts 2:30). Finally, Moses himself, to whom the books of the Law (Genesis, Exodus, Leviticus, Numbers, and Deuteronomy) are attributed, was acknowledged as a prophet (Deuteronomy 34:10).

For Peter to say that "all the prophets testify" about Jesus is a dramatic proposition. He is not gathering together a handful of verses from Isaiah and Zechariah, saying, "See, these are messianic prophecies. They refer to the Christ and are fulfilled by Jesus." Rather, Peter makes the bold claim that "all the prophets" testify about Christ. Given what "all the prophets" might include—the Law books, books we think of as history, things written by David, as well as all the books we identify as "the prophets"—we might conclude that the entire Old Testament testifies about Christ.

Jesus himself encouraged that conclusion. After his resurrection, Jesus explained to his disciples "that everything written about me in the law of Moses, the prophets, and the psalms must be fulfilled" (Luke 24:44). The whole Old Testament canon points to him.

That Peter uses the present tense of *testify* is noteworthy. The testimony of "all the prophets" is not a thing of the past. Those prophets are past, but they "testify about him" in the present: they, along with Jesus' new generations of witnesses, the apostles in Peter's day, and you and me today.

SALVATION IN TIME AND SPACE
Colossians 3:1-4

It is important to get things in the proper order. If I am studying the history of the Civil War, it is not enough for me to know what the major events were; I must have a clear sense of the order in which those events happened; otherwise I will not fully understand them. If I am assembling a bicycle or a piece of furniture, it is necessary that I follow the instructions in order, otherwise my final product will not likely be what it should be. If I am baking a cake, I cannot change the order of when I add, mix, and bake, or my dessert will be a disaster.

The issue of proper order is an important one for us as we consider what Paul wrote to the Colossians. "So if you have been raised with Christ," he wrote, "seek the things that are above."

We may have misunderstood the order of our salvation. For many of us, we naturally think in terms of our Christian lives here on earth preceding our death and our resurrection. However, in Paul's paradigm, our Christian living actually follows our death and resurrection. We die, then we are raised, and then we live with, for, and in Christ.

This is a matter that Paul explains earlier in Colossians. In 3:1, he is referring back to a more detailed discussion in Chapter 2. Simply put, Paul points to the occasion of baptism as the occasion "when you were buried with [Christ]" and "were also raised with him" (2:12).

We tend to think of Christ's resurrection as the guarantee of our own resurrection after we have died (1 Corinthians 15:20-22). Paul, however, wants us to understand that Christ's resurrection initiates the beginning of new life for us here and now. So Easter marks a happy beginning for us: the beginning of new life in Christ here on earth.

The larger theme of Paul's counsel to the Colossians, then, is about that new, reoriented life. Where once the magnet on our compass pointed to this world and to the things of this world, our new life in Christ involves a polar shift.

The same theme is articulated in Jesus' Sermon on the Mount. He instructed his followers to change their investment strategies, focusing on riches in heaven rather than riches on earth (Matthew 6:19-21). He told them to keep the kingdom primary rather than the needs of life in this world (Matthew 6:31-33). He taught them that they should live to please a divine rather than a human audience (Matthew 6:1-6).

The theme of a reoriented life is also developed in other epistles. Paul encouraged the Romans to view themselves as dead to sin but alive to God (Romans 6:11). Likewise, he warned them not to be conformed to this world but to be transformed (Romans 12:2). James cautioned that a person can be a friend with the world or a friend with God, but not both (James 4:4). John urged the Christians under his care to wean themselves from the things of this world in order to be devoted entirely to God and his will (1 John 2:15-17).

Here, Paul urged the Christians in Colossae to focus on "things that are above" rather than on "things that are on earth." That change cuts across the grain of our fallen humanity, for the things we covet and the things we consume are the things that are on earth. What we require for our basic needs and what we desire for our pleasures are things that are on earth. Our incentives, our affections, and our cravings are all tied to things that are on earth. Peeling our attention away from the earth is a struggle against our very nature.

Here we return to the time line of salvation. The things of this earth are part of our past, before we died and were raised with Christ. Paul urges the Colossians to turn their attention to their future: "above, where Christ is, seated at the right hand of God."

Finally, there is a personal component to Paul's picture of the Christian life. Our call is not to follow a cold and impersonal law. Rather, our lives are all about a person: Jesus Christ. We are raised with him, he is our life, our life is hidden with him, and we navigate our living by looking to where he is. We do not follow the precepts of a dead teacher. We live in, with, and toward the risen Lord.

COME, SEE, GO, TELL
Matthew 28:1-10

I wonder if angels ever need to sit down. I know that I need to, but I somehow doubt that angels ever need to sit. That this angel sat on the stone after rolling it away, therefore, strikes me as a symbol of victory. The stone that once sealed Christ's grave was reduced to an impromptu bench.

In Mark's account of the women's visit to the tomb, the women worried about who would roll away the stone for them (Mark 16:3). What was massive and immovable for them proved to be a small matter for the angel. Likewise, the burden that was too great for us—death—was altogether conquered by Christ. We could not roll away that stone by ourselves; but like the women, we come to the grave and find that it is already rolled away for us.

We cannot help but admire these women. The male followers of Jesus were apparently sitting at home, wallowing in their fear and grief. These women, however, had a love for Christ that manifested itself in action: they went to the tomb to care properly for his corpse.

Then, when they arrived, the women distinguished themselves again. An angel appeared on the scene in what can only be described as a spectacular arrival: an earthquake, a discarded boulder, the brilliance of lightning, and the bright whiteness of snow. The male guards, probably seasoned soldiers with weathered faces, trembled and fainted at the sight of the angel. The women, however, remained standing. While the strong soldiers lay unconscious on the ground, the women stood upright and listened to the angel.

Interestingly, the rolling away of the stone was not concurrent with Christ's resurrection. The angel rolled away the stone and then promptly reported, "He is not here; for he has been raised, as he said ... Come, see the play where he lay." Moving the stone was not for Christ to get out, but for the women to get in. The stone did not have to be removed for the resurrection; it had to be removed for proof of the resurrection.

We noted earlier that the arrival of the angel must have been a fantastic spectacle. Virtually every time an angel appears to a human being in Scripture, his first words are what they are here: "Do not be afraid." Far from the cute and harmless connotation we have given to "cherubic" and "angelic," the fact that angels have to say, "Do not be afraid" should give us some sense of the awesomeness of an angelic visage.

And yet, for all the rumble and radiance of the angel's arrival, it turns out to be only the second feature. The truly big event has already occurred: Jesus has risen.

As far as we can tell, Christ's resurrection occurred without fanfare. The women did not see it. The angel had not arrived on the scene yet. The guards were outside the tomb, passing the time, while on the inside their dead charge was quietly coming back to life and disappearing.

The audience part of us would like for Easter to have been a show, a big production with a heavenly spotlight. Instead, Christ quietly escaped death and the grave without being noticed. That may disappoint us, but it should not surprise us. After all, his arrival in the world was similarly without fanfare. We cherish the familiar tableau of shepherds, angels, and wise men, but the reality is that the Son of God came into the world mostly unnoticed by the world.

From beginning to end, Jesus opted out of the spotlight. His birth took place in a barn out back of a little town. His ministry was marked by multitudes, but he seemed always to deflect rather than embrace attention (Mark 7:36; Luke 5:14; John 6:14-15). He did not respond to the mockers' challenge to prove himself by coming down from the cross (Matthew 27:42), and he did not rise from the grave publicly. His glory, it seems, is yet to be revealed (Colossians 3:4).

So the Gospels do not end with a happy ending. We do not witness the glory of the Resurrection, followed immediately by the curtain closing. Rather, the women are invited to witness the emptiness of the tomb, and then instructed to "go quickly and tell."

This is the great post-Resurrection command. Time and again during his ministry, Jesus specifically instructed folks not to tell about him (Matthew 16:20; 17:9; Mark 7:36; Luke 8:56). On this side of the empty tomb, however, the instruction changes. Now it is time to tell.

If the quintessential fairytale ending is "they lived happily ever after," then the quintessential Gospel ending is "go and tell." The angels instruct the women to go and tell the disciples that Jesus had been raised; shortly after, Jesus himself gives the same instruction. A similar direction is given by Jesus in John (20:17). At the end of Matthew and Mark, Jesus' final words to his disciples are to go and tell (Matthew 28:19-20; Mark 16:15); and Peter references that commandment in his speech at Cornelius' house (Acts 10:42).

Easter is not a happy ending; it is a happy beginning. The happy ending for which our loving God longs is that none should perish but all come to repentance.

So the story continues after Easter. We leave the empty tomb, raised with Christ, our minds set on things above, to go and tell.

How is your life different because Christ is risen?

How else should your life be different because Christ is risen?

The women and the apostles had a clear understanding after Easter of who they were to tell and what they were to tell. What does God want you to tell? and to whom?